ARREST
AND EXILE

Why heap curses upon Russia? . . .

This is a Slav quarrel, an old family affair

*Already judged by Fate, and not one of you is
    capable of solving it.*

*It is an old struggle in which alternately we
    yield one to the other.*

*Who will win? the haughty Pole or the sturdy
    Russian?*

*Will all the Slav brooks unite in the Russian
    sea?*

*Leave us alone! You know nothing of these
    bloody pages of our history,*

*You have neither understanding nor sympathy
    for our family quarrels.*

*. . . they have no meaning for you and the
    only thing that stirs you*

Is the useless courage of the desperate conflict.

PUSHKIN

ARREST AND EXILE

The true story of an American woman in Poland and Siberia 1940-41 by Lilian T. Mowrer, *author of "Journalist's Wife," with a foreword by* Olga Kochanska

WILLIAM MORROW & COMPANY, NEW YORK, 1941

AN UNCOMMON VALOR REPRINT EDITION
Printed in the United States of America

ISBN: 979-8869046659

for

MY SISTER IN LONDON

this story of another woman

who could "take it."

FOREWORD

Now back, safe in Chicago, memories of Siberia are like an evil dream.

Safe! That's a conception difficult for Americans in the United States to understand. They are so accustomed to security that they have lost even the sense of danger. But in today's Europe such is not the case. Personal security is becoming ever more threatened.

I am a musician, not a writer. I can relate the story of my arrest and imprisonment in Siberia, but I never could have written it—the loneliness, the terror and heartbreak of those long months. Therefore I was pleased and gratified when Lilian Mowrer said she would work with me and write my story. Mrs. Mowrer knew Poland, Russia, and the Russians. As an experienced journalist she had every qualification for the work; as a sympathetic, warm-hearted friend she could understand my point of view and enter into my emotional experience. Yet, I wondered a little if anyone, even the author of *Journalist's Wife*, could actually tell my story as it really happened without any loss of reality. Even when I was visiting Mrs. Mowrer in Washington and, with her as a companion, living through hour after hour, day after day, with her patient but relentless searching for every detail, not only of events but of my inner thoughts and reactions, even then I wondered—

Then she sent me the first few chapters, and I stopped wondering. As I read on I found myself back again in Lemberg, I heard the iron-shod footsteps of my Russian captors; then those long days in the freight car bound for Siberia, then those months a prisoner. It was all as though Lilian Mowrer had been my constant companion and confidant through that whole period of my life.

I cannot pay Mrs. Mowrer's skill as a writer and an interpreter any higher tribute than to declare that my story as here told is true in the complete and ultimate sense of the word.

And here, too, I want to thank all the people in that prison camp who were so kind to me, and who rejoiced at my ultimate release without a trace of envy or bitterness. They made me realize again how fine and unselfish human beings can be and how much they can help each other. If my adopted country, Poland, has such people to build her up again after this war is over I know she will again take her place among the great nations of the world.

OLGA KOCHANSKA

Chicago
August 20, 1941

CONTENTS

ARREST
AND EXILE

1. ARREST

At two o'clock in the morning of June 29, 1940, three figures could be seen stealthily picking their way through the hilly parkland of one of the residential sections of the romantically beautiful city of Lemberg.* The moon was still bright in the sky as they turned into the Obrony Lwowa Ulica, and the trees surrounding the tall houses threw sharp shadows on the sidewalks as the men crept along peering up at the numbers on the buildings. Deep silence reigned, a tomblike hush unnatural in a Polish city this size. There was no echo of footsteps from some belated reveller; no taxi hooted in the distance of the downtown theatre section around the Plac Halicki where sidewalk cafés usually collected a lively, chattering throng after the evening shows. Not even the rumble of market carts coming in from the country with their piles of cabbage, turnips and carrots broke the stillness of that summer night.

The citizens of Lemberg had been warned that they might expect an air raid and had been ordered to re-

* German name of the city of Lwow.

main in their homes with the blinds drawn and all lights extinguished. And though it was nine months now since the Russians had invaded their country, and there had been no attacks or fighting in the town since their arrival, the townspeople did not dare disobey.

"So now we know where to find them all," said Shura, the leader of the three men, winking at the others, "and the threat of a raid puts them into a proper attitude of fear and makes it easier for us to deal with them."

He liked to give his companions tidbits of information like this, for he was a conceited fellow and felt immensely superior to all of them; *he* had seen service in a foreign country once before, while this was the first time they had ever been outside Russia.

They halted before the high walls of Number 16 and Shura pulled the bell with a violent jerk to show how very important he was. They did not have long to wait. A trembling little man fumbling at the buttons of his greatcoat, which he had hastily thrown over his nightshirt, was soon standing before them, timidly asking them what they wanted.

"Kochanska . . . Olga Kochanska, does she live here?" demanded Shura.

"Up on the third floor," whispered the man, leading the way to the main stairway of the apartment building and turning on the electric light in the hall. "The door on the right."

The three men stalked off without a word and mounted the low, wide staircase, their feet clattering on the uncarpeted stairs and making an unwonted echo through the building.

They rang the front doorbell and could hear its faint tinkle through the apartment. Nothing happened for a long time, then a light appeared for a moment as someone inside lifted the cover from a circular peephole in the door. An eye peered at them, then all was dark and silent again.

"She certainly takes her time opening," grumbled Shura, spitting on the wainscoting and pushing furiously at the bell once more.

Olga Kochanska sat up in bed, her hand clutching her throat in fear as the bell rang a third time. Dora, the maid, came into the room, an electric torch in her hand. For thirty-six years this sturdy little brown-faced woman had served her mistress with the doglike devotion of a Polish peasant. This loyalty she extended to everyone connected with the family, so deeply did she feel the solidarity of the clan; and for Olga, the guest in the house, she was up and dressed, ready to face whatever terrors the night visit might bring.

"What is it?" asked Olga, although in her heart she guessed what the summons meant, and she knew why the old woman was shaking and crying. All last night she had had a premonition of what was going to happen. Even her dreams had been filled with dread grey shapes that threatened her and compassed her about.

"Whoever can be at the door this time of night?" she repeated, as thundering knocks now followed the sound of the bell.

Dora gulped, wringing her hands and twisting the front of her full flowered skirt.

"It is the Russian police, *pani* Kochanska," she whispered, her mouth quite dry with the fear that was in her, and her breath coming in painful little gasps. "I looked through the spyhole. I had heard them coming up the stairs and I got up to see who it could be. There are three of them, with revolvers in their hands. What shall we do? Oh, what shall we do?"

"Let them in," said Olga dully, sitting up and feeling around with her bare feet for the slippers that were somewhere at the side of the bed. Dora stood irresolutely wiping her tears, her eyes full of apprehension; but the furious banging at the door roused her to action, and taking a bathrobe from a hook on the door and handing it to Olga, she went out of the room and into the front hall.

Her hands shook so she could hardly unfasten the heavy chain and draw back the bolts, but she opened the door at last, holding it wide as for honored guests.

"*Prosze panów*," her old lips muttered, "how can I serve your honors?"

The three men brushed past her and strode into the hall, staring about them with arrogant looks. They were all young and wore the blue peaked cap, the blue trousers striped with light red, and the belted khaki tunic of the Russian Home Office uniform, (the Narodnyi Kommissariat Wnutrenngx Del) whose members, known as the N.K.W.D., now took the place of the dreaded O.G.P.U. although there was little, except the name, changed in their function or sinister power.

Dora followed them with fear-widened eyes, but even in her panic she did not forget that the police needed watching closely. There were all kinds of valuable knickknacks lying around the house, and she had noted how their eyes coveted the costly objects and how they moved stealthily around with obvious intention of pocketing something. When Shura directed her curtly to bring him to Olga she ushered all three into the bedroom so she could keep an eye on them and see that they would not steal.

Olga was standing in the middle of the room, very slim and tall in her white bathrobe.

"You are Olga Kochanska?" asked Shura abruptly, hardly looking at her.

"Yes," she answered, striving to keep her voice calm in spite of her wildly beating heart.

"You are to dress at once and come with me."

"Now? . . . At this time? But what for?"

"Orders."

"But where are you taking me?"

"You applied for permission to go to Warsaw, didn't you?"

"Yes. I have property there, and I want to go . . . ."

"Well, we're taking you to Warsaw," broke in the man, cutting short all explanations. "Make haste; you're to come at once."

"But I think there must be some mistake," protested Olga; "surely you are making an error. I am an American citizen. I unfortunately have not my passport with me, but I have a letter concerning it from the American Embassy in Moscow." She handed him the letter, the precious letter telling him all about it, stating that a new American passport was being issued . . . that it would be ready in three months. He hardly glanced at the letter. Something in the quick way that he averted his eyes made her wonder if he really knew how to read.

"Couldn't you take me to the headquarters of the N.K.W.D in Lemberg?" she begged. They could read the letter there. They would surely realize that there had been a mistake, that she could not be expected to leave like this, at a moment's notice, for a journey to Warsaw where she might have to spend many weeks.

"You are to come with me," shouted Shura, impatient at her resistance. "Now make haste; pack what you need; you can't take much. We must be off at once." He seemed to tower over her, compelling her against her will. Dora fetched some suitcases, and together the two women began nervously taking clothes and linen out of closets and drawers.

"You can only take what you can carry," remarked the guard, observing the piles laid out on the bed. His hectoring tone threw the women into fresh confusion and their indecision was increased by Shura's constant cry of "Faster, faster, we have no time to lose."

Dora began to whimper and Olga looked around her in despair. There was so little time for packing; there was so little space. What should she take? It would be hot in Warsaw. Olga put in a little black silk dress, and a blue printed one; two white piqué frocks and a well-cut brown woollen skirt, a present from an American friend. To the underwear she added a pair of stout shoes, also a gift from the American's wardrobe. "Heaven knows how much walking around I shall have to do in Warsaw, I'd better take some comfortable shoes," she thought. She rolled a light summer topcoat in a small plaid rug and put a strap round it. "Will you kindly leave the room while I dress?" she asked the guards.

"We'll be waiting right outside," Shura responded. "Now, no tricks, mind."

"I will make *zrobie pani* some tea," said Dora, putting the rug on top of the suitcase and going toward the kitchen.

"No, you won't. You'll not leave the room," declared Shura. He kept a sharp watch on both of them, even following Olga to the bathroom, though he made no attempt to enter. They were both weak with nervousness before everything was ready and hardly able to keep from crying, but he made them carry the luggage themselves when they left the apartment.

"I can't think what they're crying about," he said to the other guards. "She said she wanted to go to Warsaw, and now we are taking her to Warsaw she weeps." He gave a short laugh, clapped one of the men on the shoulder and they all guffawed loudly as they clattered downstairs.

It was already light when they reached the street. The men marched quickly, their heavy boots clomping on the pavement and the women made scurrying little steps, trying to keep up with them. They turned into the wide Kochanowskiego Ulica, one of the main thoroughfares, where scores of big trucks were drawn up by the sidewalk.

Those same trucks had been there the night before.

It was the sight of the trucks that had filled Olga with a terrible premonition. For a week the Russians had been deporting Polish citizens. There had been veritable man-hunts through the city. The unfortunate victims were rounded up, herded into trucks, and driven to the station. No one knew why they were taken, where they were sent, or whatever happened to them.

"But they will surely never deport women," thought Olga, trying to allay the rising tide of terror within her.

"They won't deport me. . . . I'm an American."

Several people with their luggage at their feet were waiting by the lorries when Olga arrived. The guards halted her beside one of them, told her to put her suitcase on the sidewalk, and bade Dora return to the house.

"But I must wait with *pani* Kochanska," begged the old woman; "she cannot stand around in the street alone."

"She won't be alone," laughed a guard, giving the old woman a little push.

"I'll bring you some tea, and something to eat while you are waiting," she whispered to Olga. "To think of you going out like this in the morning without a bite. . . ."

"You'll do nothing of the sort," shouted the guard. "Now . . . you beat it."

Dora hovered around for a few minutes, but the guard's attitude became so menacing that she finally crept away. But in a short time she was back again. "I've brought you these," she whispered, bending down to unfasten the suitcase and slip into it a little package and an enamel cup and a case with a spoon and fork in it. "You may need them on the trip . . . you never know." She tried to kiss Olga's hand, but once again the guard shooed her away.

All the time crowded lorries, driven by uniformed men, dusty and travel-stained, evidently coming from out of town, were arriving and depositing their human loads on the sidewalk. Here some eight or ten men in city clothes, and working in their shirt sleeves, were sorting the people according to lists they held in their hands, directing some to the N.K.W.D. offices just around the corner, ordering others into the waiting trucks which were driven off in the direction of the station, shouting at the children who were crying with fright at all the noise and confusion, threatening the adults with violent and angry gestures.

Olga watched with dismay heart-rending scenes as men bade farewell to their wives, or women were bundled along in one direction by guards who refused to let their men accompany them.

Four soldiers with revolvers thrust in their belts and rifles over their shoulders marched up and down the street, herding the crowds closer and seeing that they did not stray away.

"*Pani* Kochanska, *pani* Kochanska!" called a voice. Olga turned and recognized Madame Prawdzik, who occupied the apartment under hers. The woman was weeping and dishevelled, and, together with her sister, was making an effort to resist the guard who was pushing her into one of the trucks.

"We can't go alone, we can't go alone," she kept crying. "And Jolas . . . Jolas . . . !" Olga knew that Jolas, Madame Prawdzik's husband, had been in hiding every night, ever since the mass deportation began. He was a Jew and was afraid he might be taken, as so many Jews had been among the first to be arrested. Each night he slept at a different address; his friends put him up or he took a room at some insignificant hotel. And now, after all his efforts, it was his wife who was being carried off and he would never know what had happened to her or where she was! "Jolas!" she wailed.

While her cries attracted everyone's attention, her sister managed to slip away from the crowd; she knew the man's hiding place, and in a short time Mr. Prawdzik appeared. He was a stout, energetic little man who brought a large roll of bedding with him, and was accompanied by a frightened-looking hotel porter carrying a suitcase. He marched up to the men on duty and in halting Russian began arguing with them, demanding that he be allowed to accompany his wife, that he too be arrested. They paid no attention to him and waved him aside, but he refused to take "no" for an answer. When he saw he could make no impression on them, he addressed himself to one of the soldiers. He pleaded, he shouted, he wheedled and pressed money on the man. Finally he took an embroidered linen handkerchief from his pocket and put it in the soldier's hand: nine months' contact with the army of occupation had given him a new sense of values. In the end he obtained what he wanted and was thrust into the truck with his wife.

Another man, his mind crazed by the horror of his fate, broke into loud, hysterical sobbing and shook his fists in the air; he cursed and threw himself violently from side to side, flecks of foam on his lips. A curly-haired boy of about two who had been holding his hand watched with grave, astonished eyes while friends sprang to his father's side to soothe and restrain him, this father whom he had only known as someone very strong and brave, who hoisted him on his shoulders when he was tired and who brought comfort, sitting by his bedside telling fairy tales when he woke screaming from a nightmare.

Passers-by, hurrying to their offices, were shocked by the sight. Some of them stopped and tried to talk to the unfortunate man. But the soldiers pushed them away, using the butt ends of their rifles to clear the streets. The motors were warming up and great clouds of black smoke sent an acrid stench over the scene. More and more men and women were being pushed into the trucks, their luggage slung in after them, and with a roar the heavy camions lurched away, to return again shortly for fresh loads.

The June sun was beginning to beat hot on the pavements and Olga shifted wearily from one foot to another. The city was slowly awakening. Shutters were thrown back and from upper windows of nearby buildings people leaned out, watching in silence and consternation the confusion of the departures.

"They are like a theatre audience at a tragic play," thought Olga. "They are moved and shocked, but they are helpless. They can do nothing."

She too began thinking of the scenes she was witnessing as something unreal. "This cannot be happening to me," she kept repeating to herself. "It isn't possible that I am going to be taken away." She struggled to hold back the overwhelming truth.

Tears filled her eyes and rolled slowly down her cheeks. "If only I had someone with me. If only I were not alone." Tears gushed quicker at the memory of that word.

She was alone. Waclaw was dead. Nothing could alter that fact. Even if the Russians let her off now and came to tell her it was all a mistake, they couldn't bring back Waclaw.

With his death her real life had ended.

All that had happened since was like a horrid dream. War, the Russian invasion, the sorrow, fear and discomfort that crowded her days, even the exile which threatened her now were like shadows compared with the awful reality of Waclaw's death.

Only a year ago she had been the adored wife of a man whom all the world knew and applauded. But his life had suddenly snapped, like a broken string on his own loved Stradivarius.

Waclaw Kochanski lay dead in the Conservatoire at Warsaw. The entire musical world mourned its loss and from every corner of the globe his pupils sent her cables and letters expressing their deep sorrow.

She had been so little prepared for the blow. And, as though the personal loss were not hard enough to bear, she had had to face the endless formalities attendant on the death of a celebrity; she had to meet and acknowledge official condolences; there were duties to perform before a new Director of the Conservatory could be appointed; declarations to make, forms to sign, questions to be answered. How could they know, those correct and cold-faced functionaries, that even words of sympathy were torture to her, stabbing her with memories too poignant to be borne? How could they guess that every time she uttered his name a knife turned in her heart?

She had fled from it all finally and hidden herself

in the country. Amid the woods and lakes of Maniewicz, far from officialdom, she tried to get command of
herself again, find courage to face the future. She did
not stay at her own property. She could not endure
the sight of that gay little villa, with its great, flowery
gardens, where she and Waclaw had spent so many
happy days. But on the nearby estate of a friendly
landowner she sought refuge in a cottage, sharing it
with a young girl whose sweet presence and sweeter
voice helped her through the worst hours of her loneliness.

Always there was soft singing about her. Lina was
like some lovely bird with a spontaneous outpouring
of song. And although at first the music opened such
floodgates of weeping that Olga was prostrate and
spent, it healed her more than she would ever have
dared to hope.

Music crept back into her life again. She had thought
that all she loved was dead forever and she could never
bear to play again. Her own violin she had left behind
in Warsaw. Since she could no longer make music with
Waclaw, never again play with him the concertos which
had been their delight, she felt her career was ended.
But Lina's singing wrought a miracle and she knew
she would be able to face the future alone.

Slowly the old ways of living reasserted themselves.
She joined her friends, sank into the easy, hospitable,
almost feudal life on the big Polish estate. There was
much coming and going those days; so many visitors
arriving from the capital, only a night's journey away.
There was anxious talk of political tension and threat
of war, but she cared for none of these things.

Death was still too personal a sentiment for her to envisage war, and death on the immense scale war would involve—such a possibility did not penetrate her consciousness. She spent her time walking in the tranquil countryside; reading the new books strewn through the rooms in the low, white, handsome house. Even when Jan, her son, kissed her good-bye to join his regiment she imagined it was the annual military manœuvres that called him away. She was still too bruised and shaken to be fully aware of all that was going on around her.

And then Poland was suddenly overwhelmed by the German invasion; the whole country seared by steel and fire. Before its valiant defenders could recover from this unexpected onslaught Soviet troops struck at their rear and what hope of resistance remained was over.

The Russians came in, and the Russians remained. Almost immediately Olga's house and property were commandeered by the N.K.W.D.; and, with her hosts, she fled from Maniewicz. Her first taste of war was their trip to nearby Kowel, where for two days they remained shut up in a box car in the station, while firing and fighting went on all around them. All means of transportation seemed to have vanished: there was a complete lack of gas for automobiles; and trains, other than occasional ones for the troops, no longer ran. So, like thousands of other refugees, she stayed in Kowel, sharing two rooms with her friends, where twelve people spread their mattresses on the sitting-room floor, and sleep was difficult and haunted by uneasy dreams. Queer, how she remembered, even now, those vibrating piano strings every night. Poor Mr. Blair coughed so dreadfully, and from his couch under the grand piano he set all the bass wires thrumming.

After a month they moved on: the Russians re-established a limited train service for civilian use. "But mind you travel third," warned a Polish official, "go 'hard,' for the first and second are already swarming with lice."

Jammed to the footboards, with men seated on the tops of carriages, that train took two days for a journey which normally would have taken only a few hours. They arrived at Lemberg in Eastern Galicia and learned for the first time that their country had been partitioned, that Germany and Russia had drawn a line of demarcation through the middle of it, and that Poland, as an independent country, no longer existed.

Olga was distraught at the sudden realization of her position. Her home and all she owned were in Warsaw, yet she found herself, without passport, papers, or money, in Soviet-occupied territory. In vain she appealed for permission to leave the city, sought to regain her American passport, applied for a visa to the United States; the endless hours of waiting and inquisitional inquiries to which she was subjected availed her nothing. Reluctantly she abandoned the idea of returning home and tried to make her life over in Lemberg. She was lucky at first, for she ran into an old friend, Vilma Gerhardt, who had been her friend in Chicago; a merry, music-loving soul, who, like herself, had later married a Pole and come to live in Poland.

Together the two women shared the discomforts of the Russian occupation, trying to meet with humor and resignation the constant surveillance, rigorous rationing, the lack of fuel and nightly curfew which the Bolsheviks imposed. Then Vilma sold her household goods and joined her relatives in Chicago. Once more without a home in the overcrowded city, Olga remembered an old friend she had known during her student days at Lemberg and sought her out. But blackened walls and a pile of débris were all that remained of Madame Ostrowska's lovely villa.

"It was bombed right at the beginning of the war," neighbours told her, "but *pani* Ostrowska has moved to an apartment not far from here."

So she had come finally to 16 Milkowskiego Ulica, where the old lady welcomed her with open arms.

"Why, this is like old times, Olga. I'll gladly take you in. I am lucky, child, I have no Russians quartered on me. They leave me alone because I teach music all day. If you could see how they live and what they do!"

That was the lament that Olga heard from everyone with Russians in their homes. She was happy she had found so congenial a living place and even hoped that she might be able to give some violin lessons, for the prospects of getting her money out of Warsaw seemed very remote.

But hardly had she begun to cope with her new existence when the sinister deportations began. No reason was ever given to the unfortunate people ordered so unceremoniously to leave their homes. At first it looked as if the Russians were merely choosing a rather brutal way of finding accommodations for their own people . . . for the troops, the officers and their wives, all the commissars, and petty bureaucrats who had flooded the city, taxing housing facilities to the utmost.

The deportations had begun on a small scale, and since the Poles looked on the Russian invasion as something temporary, and as the Russians at first did everything to allay suspicion, no undue alarm was felt when certain "enemies of the new State" were removed.

But gradually the number of deportees increased, extending to officers, magistrates, civil servants, irrespective of political affiliations. It looked like a systematic dispersal of the Polish population, particularly the more influential and wealthy classes; and as Olga stood on the sidewalk that hot morning at the end of June she realized that the crowds beside her represented a cross section of the town's leading citizens.

When she reached the Podzamcze station, she was horrified to see the numbers already assembled there, and who, throughout the long day, continued to arrive at regular intervals and leave in the overcrowded trains. Evidently a very thorough round-up was being made in every quarter of the town.

She stood at the back of the platform, pushed and jostled by the thousands of luckless individuals waiting there: children were crying, men and women were moving desperately through the surging mass, some intent on tracing a missing member of their group or family, others struggling to recover their luggage, which was continually swept aside in the general confusion. Soviet officials seemed unable to cope with the situation, and made no attempt to establish order.

The heat was insufferable, and because it had been so fresh when she left home, Olga was wearing a woollen dress, a sweater and coat. Now she was overcome by the sun which poured through the glass roof of the station. Looking wildly about her to see if she was being watched, she struggled to the waiting room, dragging her heavy suitcase with her. The place was crowded, and a Soviet official was standing at the door. He made no attempt to stop her as she went in, though he looked at her very closely.

Harassed families were frantically rearranging hastily packed baggage, and the whole place was strewn with personal belongings; one or two women were trying to hide valuables in their underwear; a girl was lying on the floor as if she had fainted, but nobody paid any attention to her; a frightened little boy was vomiting in one corner, while his distraught mother was vainly trying to hush a screaming infant. Three children, playing with their dolls, were seated on the shiny, hard black seat running round the room.

"I shall come and arrest you," said the first.

"No, *I* shall arrest *you*," retorted the second. "I am the secret police."

"You couldn't arrest anyone, you're too small," said the third.

"Oh, no, I'm not. I'm the p'lice. The secret p'lice can do anything," insisted the little girl.

Olga pushed her way into a corner and slipped into a light dress, squeezing the other things into her stuffed suitcase. She left the waiting room and went into the buffet, but she could not swallow a mouthful; the food seemed to choke her. She wrapped up some rolls and put them in her handbag, then hurried back to the station platform.

Outside the station there was a continuous uproar as truckload after truckload arrived. There was no room in the station-yard for all the traffic: women's screams rose above the honking of horns and purr of motors as chauffeurs of newly arriving cars plunged into the human medley, overturning baggage and nearly crushing the people who made a wild rush to get out of the way.

Inside, heavy freight trains, belching smoke and steam, drew up to the platform from time to time, and a man or woman in N.K.W.D. uniform read out a long list of names. These people, clutching their belongings, were bundled into the box cars and their trek into the unknown began. The shouting and shoving increased in violence, and with each departure the tide of human misery mounted higher. For, whether by design or carelessness, many families were broken up and sent off in different trains. Olga witnessed the most frantic leave-takings: one mother was carried senseless into the car after being torn from a boy who could not have been more than twelve and who was left behind to follow on a later train alone. There were cries and appeals; last minute efforts to establish some means of future communication, final frantic redistribution of suitcases and packages.

For nobody knew where he was going.

It was this torturing uncertainty that constituted the greatest suffering; the desperate Poles begged to be told where they were being sent, but the Russians either shrugged their shoulders with indifference, or curtly refused to answer such requests.

Olga herself applied to one of the officers directing the exodus and explained in detail the circumstances of her case, insisting that she could not possibly be included among these groups to be sent away. She implored him to let her apply at the N.K.W.D. headquarters, where, she felt sure, there would be records of her correspondence with the American Embassy in Moscow.

But all without result. Either he would not or he could not take the responsibility of releasing her.

"When you reach your destination you will be able to take up the whole matter with the commander in charge," was all he would promise. "No doubt things will be straightened out. But since you filed an application to go to Warsaw, that is undoubtedly where you are being taken."

Olga looked at him wrathfully and with complete distrust. This was the kind of quibbling and maddening insistence on bureaucratic detail she encountered everywhere under the occupation: it seemed to flourish in inverse ratio to its ability to get things done; and she wondered if, in dealing with their own nationals, the Bolsheviks combined the same callous attitude with the same administrative chaos.

Like all Poles, Olga was inclined to despise Russians, but like the rest of her compatriots, she had never looked upon them as enemies.

The only enemy Poland knew was Germany. Indeed, at the first occupation of their country many Poles accepted the official explanation that the Russians had come only to save White Russian and Ukrainian minorities from the Germans.

It was difficult at first for the Poles to consider seriously these hordes who marched into their city; and their contempt for the new proletariat state grew greater when they saw at close quarters how most of its inhabitants lived. With the coming of the Russians the whole aspect of the city changed. The dirty, tattered bed linen which the newcomers hung to air at the windows seemed a fitting banner of the Soviet régime and a symbol of its achievement.

A barbaric note too was added by the thousands of dark-skinned troops who poured in from the furthest reaches of the Asiatic Soviets: hook-nosed Lesghians in flowered cotton prints; turbaned Tartars from Dagestan in full-skirted tunics and bloomers caught tightly at the ankle; Caucasian mountaineers; wild, magnificent-looking creatures in spite of their dirt. They drove herds of cattle through the main thoroughfare—the broad Akadamicka Ulica—as unconcernedly as though still in their native villages. Nothing shocked the Poles more than this sight, for the intruders did not walk like white men; but proceeded at the loping little dogtrot of a Chinese coolie, their toes turned in, like all horsemen.

Sloe-eyed, slatternly women carrying babies wrapped in heavy, soiled quilts stared open-mouthed at the magnificent cathedral, the Renaissance palaces, the flowered walks and imposing public buildings. That they were unaccustomed to such sights was only too evident in their bearing and conversation. They had been told that the Poles lived in misery under a régime of ruthless capitalistic exploitation, yet they encountered an ease, luxury and abundance their savage lives had never known.

Life in Lemberg went on in a kind of horrible caricature of the former happy days. Wealthy citizens walked in fear while the invaders, in commandeered automobiles, filled the city with rapturous honking and tooting, driving like excited children with a reckless disregard for lampposts, flowerbeds, and pedestrians.

Shopkeepers told strange stories of the superstitious awe with which their new customers regarded even the most ordinary commodities: much they had never seen before and did not know its use. Women purchased showy upholstery goods for gowns, and at dressmaker's fittings revealed dirty bare bodies beneath dresses destitute of underwear; grown men clutched at novelties, broke them and discarded them. Watches they prized above all else, army officers pinning two and three at a time on their tunics like decorations: what most astonished them was the ticking, until Red commissars felt moved to explain that watches which worked were merely an insidious form of bourgeois propaganda.

The spectacle of a free economy, one which did not aim at making the people completely dependent upon the régime even in their daily household existence, was proving very disturbing, and the Soviet radio redoubled its efforts to prove the superiority of Russian economics and the Russian way of life.

Hastily the invaders seized the control of administration: jobs changed hands in a topsy-turvy nightmare.

As director of the great Politechnic, the School of Technology and the city's pride, the Russians appointed a Red Army sergeant, a student who had not even completed his studies; commissars appeared at all the schools to censor textbooks and courses; the faculties of Law, Philosophy, and Theology were suppressed at the University, where an altar to Stalin, with accompanying red lamp, was substituted for a statue to the Blessed Virgin.

Though the clergy at first escaped persecution, such heavy taxes were imposed on many of the churches that the diocese could not possibly meet them, so, for "purely administrative reasons," the churches were closed.

The theatres and movies remained open, their elegant interiors immediately sullied by the unkempt crowds who gleefully watched the shows; the Opera House played nightly with Russian or Ukrainian singers and ballet-dancers replacing Polish artists who swelled the vast ranks of unemployed. The audience gaped at the richness of the décor, the magnificence of the building; and some of the Russian women, unaccustomed to personal luxury of any kind, appeared in silk and satin nightdresses, imagining that such dainty apparel was the correct attire for these gala performances. Few Poles deigned to appear at such occasions: they were incensed at the dilapidated appearance of their beautiful theatres and the precipitate decline in the living standard which the Russian invasion entailed.

How they despised these ignorant intruders, whose primitive ways belied at every turn their boasted new order. When the inhabitants of Lemberg hurried through the streets they pretended not to hear or to understand the loudspeakers installed at every public square, blaring forth the merits and advantages of Soviet rule; they ignored the parade of military might as Soviet tanks and mechanized equipment went rolling through the town on its way to conquest; nothing could

shake their conviction that the Russian would fight
as incompetently as he did everything else.

For it became daily more apparent that it was the
Russians themselves who were dazzled and impressed
by everything they encountered in this first glimpse
of life beyond their own borders, and that what amazed
them most was that peoples existed who did not have
to be dragooned into accepting their government.

"You could travel?" asked these Muscovites incredulously, eager to hear more from the Poles of a brave
new world, so strangely unlike their own. "You could
go where you liked . . . to France? To Italy?" Such
freedom was beyond their comprehension. "*And you
came back?*" they added with even more wonderment,
revealing in a phrase their true feelings.

Although the immediate arrival in Lemberg and the
subsequent opening of the *Bakalia,* low-priced co-operatives, brought a certain amelioration in the food situation, the momentary abundance soon vanished, and
fats, meat, and sugar became as difficult to obtain as
before. Trade was carried on normally at first, as long
as the stocks held out, with Polish currency, on a par
with the rouble, as legal tender. Private trading was encouraged and soon the Russians had all the goods and
the Poles all the zlotys. Then, suddenly, just before Christmas, the zloty was withdrawn from circulation, destroying at a blow the humble remnants of well-
being of thousands throughout the city. It meant almost complete pauperization for a large section of the
country. Prices rose steeply, so that a pound of potatoes
cost three roubles, and meat anywhere from ten to fifteen roubles a pound, while leather was practically

priceless and a pair of shoes could not be bought for less than five hundred roubles. As the average worker's monthly wage was 150 roubles, the Poles began seriously to doubt the blessings of this "Government of peasants and workmen."

As months went by, news, too, began to trickle back from those men who had volunteered to go to Russia and work in the Don basin. They were appalled at the standard of labour conditions they encountered there and the hardships under which free workmen were supposed to live. It was like a penal colony. The inhabitants of Lemberg resisted as much as possible any further efforts of "Russification," clinging to their own passports and declining the Soviet "identity books" although lack of these made jobs increasingly difficult to obtain. They watched with increasing concern the wholesale plunder of the city's movable goods and property, the railway workshops, equipment and furniture of the banks and factories; and submitted resentfully to all the arbitrary orders and often contradictory measures which reduced everything to chaos and slowly deprived them of their private property and means of business.

Their Mayor, their member of Parliament, Mr. Sommerstein, and various municipal authorities were early arrested, and replaced by Russian candidates with an administration modeled on Soviet lines.

Nor were the Russians content with this: it would seem that Stalin had a morbid craving for approval and so elections were inaugurated, a kind of farcical plebiscite by which the Poles were allowed to vote as to the precise manner in which their country should be annexed to the U.S.S.R. Everyone was urged to the polls, in this "entirely and completely free" plebiscite; even the sick and crippled were brought on stretchers, and when it was really impossible for someone to leave his home, the ballot box was brought to the bedside. Blank returns were counted as favorable to the government, and, from the very moment of its inception, there was no doubt as to the outcome of results.

Once all the occupied Polish territories were formally incorporated into the federated States of the U.S.S.R., the Russians abandoned their kid-glove methods of dealing with the inhabitants. They openly exploited animosities between peasants in the Ukraine and those in the rest of the occupied territory, which they insisted on calling "Western Ukraine" in spite of its Polish character. All kinds of old grievances were revived and encouraged. In an effort to wean these agricultural workers from their former landlords, the Soviet authorities made the most tempting promises; and, dazzled by gifts of land and prospects of autonomy, the Ukrainian peasants welcomed the new régime with open arms. But their joy was short-lived: first they found that the milk and grain and everything they produced was all for their new masters; and then, in one of the characteristic and bewildering changes, their newly granted land was all collectivized and became State property. "Take back your freedom," grumbled the Ukrainians. "Return to us our slavery," they demanded, when they found out that the distribution of land was an illusion.

Disillusioned, too, were the Ukrainians in city jobs who were given "favored nation" privileges at first. The porter in Madame Ostrowska's apartment house had been proudly installed by his Russian masters; but "I would kiss the ground of a free Poland," he confessed to Olga unhappily, not six months later.

"It's all fraud and deception everywhere! Such inefficiency and muddle!" mused Olga, almost fainting with exhaustion, ready to weep at the long hours of waiting and the lack of any food. She had been standing since four in the morning and it was now late afternoon. She marveled that she could stand such treatment, that she did not redouble her protests, demand explanations, make a scene. She wondered why all the others about her accepted so passively this monstrous disruption of their private lives.

Olga was not given to introspection: hers was an artist's nature, intuitive, sensitive, with little logical coherence. But though reluctant to dissect her thoughts and feelings she was aware that there was a reason for this spineless acquiescence on her part. She guessed why she submitted to this dragooning.

She was afraid.

Exactly what she was afraid of she did not know. But she felt she was in the clutches of some horrifying machine and she did not dare challenge its power.

As the sunlight deepened and cast long shadows through the glass roof, a well-dressed woman approached and spoke to her. "You look so worn and lonely," she murmured sympathetically. "Do you belong among these unfortunates? Won't you let me help you?"

Tears sprang into Olga's eyes. "Oh, I couldn't think of troubling you," she began.

"Listen, you could easily slip away from here," went on the woman. "I can help you escape. There are hardly any guards around at present, and in this crowd anyway they would not notice you. Leave your suitcase and come with me. I'll return for it later. I have a little house outside Lemberg and I can take care of you till you can join your friends."

Her voice was so sweet and friendly that Olga's heart ached at the sound.

But she dared not accept.

"I cannot. I cannot," she cried wildly. "I should only bring you grief and trouble. If you helped me to escape they might take you in my place."

Suddenly her fears became articulate. At the woman's offer her memory stirred with all she had heard of the dread hostage system, whereby innocent victims paid for another's shortcomings; in a flash she remembered the methods of blackmail, trickery, and reprisal which held a whole nation enchained; she thought of that inhuman espionage and vigilance which never ceased once the N.K.W.D. had you in its clutches. She was afraid. More afraid than ever. But she was determined neither to fall into the snare of *agents provocateurs,* nor to involve others in her plight.

The woman left her, but returned shortly with a parcel in her hands. "I've brought you some food," she whispered. "You can surely take that from me."

Gratefully Olga pressed her hand, weeping that she had ever suspected the offer, stammering her thanks. And then the unknown woman was swallowed in the crowd and Olga felt doubly alone.

Finally her turn came on the roll call. She started

and shuddered as the officer read out her name. She had long since ceased to believe that her destination would be Warsaw.

The train—a seemingly endless stretch of cars—drew up to the platform: it was composed of cattle trucks, more like prison cells than accommodations for passengers. The sides were high, with gratings near the top, and inside they were dark and fetid. There were no seats and they were far from clean. Olga found herself standing at the entrance of one of them, pushed forward by the immense press of those who had been assigned with her.

"But . . . I am being pushed under the rails. . . . I cannot possibly get in . . . the step is too high!" she cried hysterically, for now that the actual moment had come she was seized with an uncontrollable panic.

"You get in," a voice behind her commanded loudly and angrily. It was late, and there were still so many to send on their way.

Pulled by a man who had already mounted, and pushed from behind by those on the platform, Olga tried to struggle up, grasping a greasy black handrail. She felt her skirt split at the hem as she strained to reach the running board and she was breathless and almost fell before she got in the car. It was a long time before everyone was accommodated; the old people had so much difficulty climbing into the train. But the doors were slammed at last—like nailing down a coffin lid. Bolts were shot into place—that was the earth on the lid. The conductor blew his whistle—too late to think of escape now.

The long journey had begun.

2. THE JOURNEY

IT was almost dark inside the car, and the air smelled sour and used-up, as though other prisoners had already been there, poisoning the gloom with their heavy sorrow. Olga peered about her uneasily. There were twenty-eight persons beside herself, nine women, thirteen men and six children, among whom the youngest was an infant in arms. They looked at each other hopelessly, with blank faces. Although the doors were shut the train did not move.

"If we tried to arrange ourselves more comfortably," said one of the passengers timidly, breaking the silence after a very long while. "If we spread out our luggage we could fix a seat. . . ."

The words brought some cohesion into the group of strangers. They no longer stared disconsolately, clutching their poor possessions, but smiled a little hopefully and began moving around gingerly in the very limited space of the car. In one corner lay a pile of old sacking and with this some of the women began wiping the grimy walls and sweeping the dust and refuse from the floor.

They put a row of suitcases against the two long sides of the car and half the travellers squatted down, thankful to be off their feet. Two rough wooden shelves, like narrow upper berths, had been rigged up on the sides and some men and two or three women with their children cautiously clambered up, wondering if the flimsy structure would support their weight. They arranged their belongings as best they could, trying not to get in each other's way.

It was impossible to sit upright, for they were too near the roof; they could not stretch out full length, for space demanded that they all sit facing the middle of the car; so they half crouched, half sprawled, their legs dangling over the edge of their scanty perch; yet, uncomfortable as they were, the relief from the long hours of standing was so great that everyone relaxed and spirits seemed to rise. They even remembered they were hungry.

Most of them had been prevented from dining in the station buffet, but nearly all had brought food with them; and when they saw some of their fellow passengers without anything to eat, all were anxious to share. It was rather a lugubrious picnic; the heat was stifling, and although they were becoming accustomed to the dark, they were still too new to their quarters to move easily. Nobody spoke much; an embarrassed constraint tied everyone's tongue.

It is not easy for persons accustomed to the amenities of civilized travel to find themselves treated as convicts in such primitive conditions. They ate in silence, yet an undercurrent of mutual sympathy was not lacking; and as the bread and meat was passed around. a

Rabbi held a loaf in his hand a moment, his eyes lifted in prayer. And the meal which began so sadly ended rather like a communion.

The train still remained standing in the station and as the evening lengthened thirst began to torment them all. At one moment, with a clanking of bolts, the door was suddenly thrown open and a Russian guard appeared in the aperture, sharply silhouetted against the light. They all stared at this sinister figure and an elderly woman angrily demanded that they be allowed to get out and buy something to drink.

"Why should we suffer so?" she protested vehemently. He looked at her apathetically.

"Suffer?" he repeated, with cold emphasis, while his eyes roamed over the huddled mass in the car. "Why should you *not* suffer? We have been suffering so for twenty-two years."

He slammed the door shut again, but somehow his despairing words robbed his hearers of the last remnants of their courage: each became immersed in his own misery and one by one they drooped wearily over their suitcases, pillowing their heads on their arms, trying vainly to sleep. And some time during the night, as they tossed uneasily in the cramped space, the train pulled out of the station.

When dawn streaked through the gratings the train was still jogging along slowly, but its occupants paid little attention to the grey light. Waking was painful and cheerless, and each clung as long as possible to the oblivion of sleep, postponing the dreadful moment of facing a new day. But gradually, as the sun grew stronger, the carload of strangers began to stir and stretch, trying to work off the stiffness of that first uncomfortable night. The women patted their hair into order, powdered their faces, straightened their clothes, tried to adjust themselves for each other's inspection in the daylight. A single thought preoccupied them all. But now it was abundantly clear that the car was of the most primitive construction; it was literally a cattle truck made over for human occupation by the addition of a few boards; of toilet facilities there was none.

The baby cried pitifully with an exhausted little wail as he turned his head from side to side, constantly moistening his tiny lips. His mother, a tall, pale girl, had fainted the night before and even now seemed on the verge of physical collapse. She was very young: this was her first child and she was too weak to nurse him. Again and again she put his mouth to her breast, but there was no milk for him, and each time she turned her head away and cried. A group of relatives hovered around her; from the corner where they all sat there was a hubbub of anxious whispering.

The Rabbi was her father, a handsome old man with a long beard, who even in the disorder of the morning maintained a rather patriarchal air, surrounded as he was by his four fine sons, his two married daughters, a brother with some little children, and his own elderly wife, a frightened-looking woman whose eyes constantly brimmed with tears, but whose lips moved obediently in prayer whenever he turned his warm, confident smile on her.

There were several family groups in the car talking in low, dejected tones among themselves, but as the long hours went by they began to exchange a little general conversation. They were far too exhausted to show much interest in each other, but it is impossible for so many people to live in such close proximity and ignore each other completely; and gradually, under the pressure of misery shared together, the formality of Polish bourgeois conventions broke down.

All the passengers came from upper middle-class professional circles; and the comfort and ease of their former lives made their present existence doubly painful.

Dr. Altberg was a physician who had lived in a fashionable suburb in Lemberg. He was a man of about fifty-two, accompanied by a much younger wife and their fifteen-year-old daughter, Kazia. His dark features were twisted with pain and he seemed to be in the depths of despair. Nothing roused him from his gloomy meditations.

Tomasz Zielinski was also a physician, probably not more than thirty-six, with a frail-looking wife and a little boy, about two and a half, with thick golden curls. The sanitary conditions of the convoy were causing him the gravest concern, but though he kept his fears to himself the presence of the two doctors was particularly reassuring to the other passengers. This trip into the unknown weighed on them all and its initial stages did nothing to allay their forebodings as to the effect on their health. Rabbi Krantz was already watching his wife with some alarm. She had been very restless and querulous all night, tossing and groaning, twitching her limbs convulsively; and since it was impossible even to turn without bumping into her neighbours, she had been a most uncomfortable bedfellow. Towards morning she fell into a heavy stupor, but her features still twitched, and from time to time she moaned.

More concerned about his personal appearance, apparently, than anything else was Ignac Stupek, former proprietor of a large tailor's establishment, a man of considerable means, the only one in the car, besides Olga, who had no family with him.

His clothes were extremely well-cut and elegant and he was depressed beyond measure at their frowzy, crumpled condition. He stood up a good deal to prevent his trousers bagging at the knees, and although the others smiled a little wanly at this pathetic attempt to preserve appearances, they all found themselves stimulated by it and made an effort to keep at least as tidy as possible.

Mr. Fischer, with his wife and son and daughter, occupied the berth opposite Olga. She had watched them on the Lemberg station platform, for she was impressed by the man's unusually cheery countenance. He was a prosperous lawyer with a most comfortable and reassuring manner. Problems never seemed half so serious when Josef Fischer took them in hand. He had been most helpful stacking the baggage, arranging it all in the most practical way; then he produced a stout piece of twine and secured the valises in the upper seats so that they did not come pounding into the backs of the unfortunate people crowded there.

He had been helped by a charming, silent little boy of about eleven, Tomasz Bromberg, the son of an industrialist from Cracow. The boy's parents had a wealthy sister in Palestine, and their one theme of conversation was the possibility of getting news to her of their plight.

The train jogged along with an endless, monotonous grinding of wheels. The passengers sat dejectedly, with memories submerged in a swamp of weariness and fear. Cinders and black smoke from the panting, straining engine sifted in through the gratings; but though it crawled so slowly, it showed no signs of stopping. No one knew how long the journey would last, and they could only guess in which direction they were travelling. The gratings let in light, but they were too high to admit anything but a view of the sky.

"Want to see, want to see," begged the little Zielinski boy. Everybody would have liked to see; the tedium was intolerable; each stared straight in front of him, tortured by his thoughts.

It was too dim to read, even supposing that anyone had brought a book. The little children were fretful and tired.

"Why can't I have my little bed?" pleaded Jan Zielinski tearfully, again and again.

Olga took the child on her knee to tell him a story, but he was too restless to listen.

"Look. We'll play ring-around-a-rosy," she said at last, climbing down into the middle of the car and lifting him to the ground. She took his hand and drew the Rabbi's grandchildren into the circle too. "Now, we'll all sing and make a ring together."

"Can you play ring-around-a-rosy in a train?" inquired Jan, clearly intrigued by such a prospect. All of his ideas on travelling had to be rapidly revised.

"You can do everything in a train," Olga assured him.

They all joined hands and moved around unsteadily: the car joggled and swayed and the easiest part of the game was the "all fall down," which the children enacted with gusto.

"Again . . . again," they demanded. It was the first happy moment on the trip.

Towards the end of the day footsteps could be heard overhead: someone was walking along the roof of the train, and Mrs. Zielinski gave a little scream as a trapdoor opened and a Russian guard peered down at them. He said nothing, but after a moment or two tossed a large tin pail into their midst.

There was an embarrassed pause. Then a young man hurled himself on it. The women averted their eyes. Truly it was possible to do everything in a train.

Afterwards it was the women's turn; and some of them stood like sentinels in a row—a veritable hedge—round one corner of the car. But later it was no easy task to empty the unlovely load through the gratings.

Dusk descended the second day and still the train made no halt. The passengers became increasingly dirty and uneasy and began to ration their provisions like victims in a siege. Olga had long since finished the sandwiches provided by her unknown friend in the station; but that was small hardship, for she was unable to swallow even a morsel of bread, so dry and swollen was her tongue.

The dust in the carriage, the sweltering heat, and a torturing thirst drove everyone to despair. A whole orchestration of misery was the baby's continuous wailing and his mother's heartbroken sobs; Jan Zielinski clamoured lustily for his "little bed" and would not be hushed. Suddenly the air was rent with piercing maniac screams—like lurid lightning leaping through a sultry atmosphere.

The Rabbi's wife choked in a torrent of hysterical weeping, banging her head wildly on the side of the car, shouting, laughing, her arms writhing wildly. Her husband caught her hands, trying to calm her with soothing words, but it soon became clear that she was beyond appeal to reason. Her mind seemed to have given way under the strain of suffering and she became more and more violent, with gestures and witless babblings discomfiting in their shameful betrayal of human dignity. The children stared and whimpered, not knowing what had happened, yet painfully affected by the ugly sight; and the others looked on shaken to the core.

All night the raucous cries, the unnatural weeping and beating hands kept everyone awake: the darkness seemed endless, devouring whole years; but gradually, towards dawn, the loud violence subsided, the lunatic glint in the old lady's eyes faded and her weary body fell over in a heavy torpor. Next day she drowsed and lay in a coma. Even the children were exhausted and unnaturally quiet; but those who had kept the long vigil were burdened with a new insidious fear. They had seen the stronghold of personality dissolve and a poor creature crumple beneath a fate too hard to bear. And each in his heart trembled at what might lie in store for him.

Late that evening—it was Friday night—Rabbi Krantz improvised a table in their midst and placed four lighted candles on it. With tranquil, unhurried gestures he drew about him a praying shawl, tied the prayer bands around his forehead and gathered the company about him in religious service.

"We have sinned, we have sinned," he intoned, "our sufferings and exile are punishment for our sins. But persecution and exile we have known before; we have suffered, atoned, and been forgiven. Confess and repent; this too will pass away: our sufferings shall not endure but will pass away."

Olga was the only Christian in the compartment. She had never frequented Jewish circles nor had she ever before witnessed Jewish communal prayer, that ritual which since the earliest exodus has brought Jews together to voice their longing for the homeland. But unfamiliar though it all was, it was impossible not to feel moved by its intensity, and she took comfort in the ceremony. An immense quiet settled on the assembly. After the harrowing episode of the previous night the Rabbi's words brought healing and renewed confidence. And when he lay aside his ritual garments and blew out the candles, the occupants of the carriage settled themselves down among all that remained to them of their earthly belongings; and slept more tranquilly than they had done since the journey began.

A grinding of wheels and the crunch of brakes applied abruptly and without warning. With a tremendous jerk the train came to a halt, throwing the passengers to the ground with the violence of its movement, shuddering and quivering like an animal spent by its long exertions.

There was a general rush to the doors, men and

women beat on the panels, struggling with the locks in their eagerness to get out. When the bolts were drawn and the light of a summer day streamed through the opening the passengers blinked and groped their way warily, remembering the steep step leading to the ground. They hobbled down, six hundred and fifty of them, their legs cramped and weakened by close confinement during four days.

It was a little country station of squared logs painted brown, surrounded by a high white picket-fence; one platform was covered with a high pointed roof; the other a mere plank running beside the rails. In the distance a cluster of wooden houses, little more than shacks, faced a rutted road deep in dust. Even in the brilliant sunshine a disquieting desolation lay over the hamlet; there was something infinitely forlorn in the way the roofs overhung the outer walls, plunging so near the ground that the windows were almost hidden and peered out like dark astonished eyes.

This was no Polish landscape. With sinking hearts the passengers realized they were in Russia even before a group of Russian peasants began clambering over the fence and slowly approached the train.

They wore drab clothes like impoverished city dwellers; the women, with shawls or berets on their heads, trailed long, dark skirts. The men were in shoddy black; all were barefooted and their garments were torn and of the poorest quality. But they were very clean, the women's white waists looked fresh, and to the travel-stained Poles they presented an enviably wholesome sight. It is an old Russian custom to meet trains with offerings of food for sale, and most of them had something hidden beneath their aprons—little green cucumbers, soggy dark bread, rough cheese, or a little milk. It was hardly ideal diet for those who had fasted so long, but there was a general rush to buy. The peasants snatched at the money eagerly, jabbering excitedly, making signs, trying to explain prices; the Poles crowded round pointing to the articles they wanted, but most of them found difficulty in eating the coarse, unsavoury fare. They were dazed and sick from continuous travel; they wandered up and down the platform, talking uneasily with one another, exchanging news of the trials of their trip.

In the car next Olga's a young woman had given birth to a child during those four terrible days. The incessant jolting after the anguish and shock of arrest had hastened her hour, and, all unattended by a doctor's care, the tiny life had forced its way into an unkind world.

Now the young mother, with her baby in her arms, was waiting her turn for the Russians to give her some milk. They did their best to fill all the bottles and cups the travellers thrust into their hands, but long before everyone was served the guards began ordering them off, threatening them with all kinds of penalties for trying to talk to the exiles, and beating them back with their rifle butts when they persisted in trying to sell their produce.

Olga had managed to get a cup of hot water. There had been no opportunity to make tea, but the hot clean taste of the water seemed better than anything she had ever drunk in her life before. Cheered and refreshed, she began looking about her. Fields and forests

stretched for miles and miles on either side of the railway tracks. It was the emptiest landscape she had ever
seen. She asked a guard the name of the village, but he
pretended not to hear her; when she asked him where
they were going he told her to get back into the train.

She was sure now she would never see Warsaw, and
began wondering where they were really going. She
could guess the direction the train had taken, and the
vast landscape appalled her. She had no time to make
inquiries; the exiles were being immediately driven
back to their cattle trucks, and after the brief freedom in the open air, the confinement was doubly irk-
some.

That glimpse, too, of the plain stretching to the wide
heavens was a grim revelation to them all.

"So they have brought us to Russia after all," whispered those who had hoped against hope that they
were only being taken to some place near the Polish
frontier. "It's such an immense country and we are
travelling so slowly it may be days and days before we
reach the town where we are to live."

Horror-stricken as they were, however, this new
viewpoint was a certain consolation, although a sombre
one. They no longer cherished the daily expectation of
an immediate end to their journey. With this psychological barrier removed, there was less disappointment;
they became more patient and resigned to the trip.

In Olga's car life began to follow a dreary routine.
Each morning, when hot bands of light fell through
the grating, the occupants stirred from their sleep, and
the day began. From the preciously preserved bottles
of water a miserly dole was measured out and hands

and faces freshened. The women swept the car each morning and tried to keep the baggage in scrupulous order.

They shared what food they had been able to buy, and they always tried to make the meal last as long as possible in those impossibly long days. The men suffered most when their tobacco gave out; their longing for a smoke was greater than their desire to eat. It was above all the enforced inactivity that they all found so trying; conversation might flourish for a moment, but it reverted almost immediately to speculation on their destination; it was filled with plaintive longings, and soon languished.

The three young people talked gravely about their schools and wondered what classes in Russia would be like. Henryk Fischer was ready for University; his sister and Dr. Altberg's daughter were seniors in High School.

"It will be queer studying with the Bolshies," they agreed, secretly finding the prospect not a little exciting.

Nights were chilly and Olga, up on her shelf, shivered in the steady draught that blew through the bars. She resented the fact that in the midst of so much real misery she should suffer the inconvenience of a common cold. Others were plagued with it too, and as the days went on new torments filled their lives, for in the dirty cars their bodies began to itch with lice.

To the women this was particularly revolting; they felt humiliated and ashamed, yet it was impossible to rid themselves of the pests.

Now that the train had cleared the Russian frontier,

the stops became more frequent, and about every twenty-four hours the passengers could count on a halt. They immediately made a rush to get water and tried to buy food; but they were not always successful. Peasants sometimes failed to meet the trains; several times they stopped at places far away from any village; only once did they pull up at a station with a regular buffet, but the chopped meat and fish on view were so unappetizing that few cared to risk eating it, though they welcomed the fresh supply of bread.

Nor was their predicament greatly alleviated, for they never knew how long the halt would last—it might be an hour, or only a few minutes. A fiendish caprice on the part of the Russians seemed to delight in keeping the travellers forever in suspense. So none ever dared wander far enough from the tracks in search of privacy which would have permitted them to shake the lice out of their clothes, for instance, or put on fresh linen.

Not the least of their sufferings was the necessity of attending to their most intimate needs in full view of the entire convoy. To Olga it was a hideous sight, this wholesale unbuttoning and squatting by the roadside. An overwhelming modesty laid iron clamps about her body. It refused to function amid such promiscuity; and swollen, and in great pain, she crept back into her corner again, hiding her face in her hands.

Even when the train made one of its rare halts at a station offering some primitive hygienic accommodations, the passengers' plight was hardly improved, for they were never sure that even there they would be unmolested. The guards would come storming into the waiting rooms and drag them off the water-closets. *"En route! En route!"* they shouted; and there was no alternative but to comply.

"Would you have us leave you behind?" they asked derisively when complaints were made at this unnecessarily heartless treatment. Yet that was precisely what did happen at one of the stopping places.

One woman risked leaving the tracks and wandered off in search of a peasant to get milk for her baby. Before she returned the train had gone. Her husband was frantic at the loss and rushed to the conductor beseeching him to stop so he could go back and find his wife.

The conductor would not hear of such a thing. "Don't worry," he told the man casually, "she'll be picked up by some other train . . . there will be others passing this way."

"But when? Where shall we meet again? How shall I know what's happening to her? And how can I look after the baby alone?" He tore at his hair in anguish. But the conductor only shrugged his shoulders indifferently, as though these questions had no meaning. Compassion seemed beyond his comprehension.

It was the tiny children who suffered most and parents' hearts were wrung as the babies drooped and grew every day paler and thinner. Sometimes there was a little milk to be had, but the guards did their best to keep the peasants from approaching the train. This was not so much for the purpose of starving their passengers as of preventing the natives from talking with anyone coming from beyond the confines of Russia.

Evidently a large measure of curiosity prompted the

peasants to make these excursions to passing trains. They were always eager for news, questioning the travellers about the towns they came from. And what was it like? And what did you do there? Half the time neither could understand the other; but there were many on the train who spoke Russian, and their impressions of the inhabitants spread rapidly among the rest.

The older peasants exhibited an extraordinary ignorance of many things. Olga listened to two who stood looking at the train with awe, and discussing the engine alongside the platform of a village station.

"But I don't understand what makes it go, there are no horses or reindeer to draw it," said one of them.

"It's steam, of course," said the other contemptuously.

"But my kettle steams at home and that doesn't go," objected the first.

"Your kettle isn't on wheels, silly!"

It was quite evident that the peasants regarded the exiles with the greatest friendliness and did their best to help them. At one station where the guards used rifle butts to keep back a group of them, one young girl crawled under the train and from the opposite side, where the guards could not see her, threw a rouble in a twist of paper into a car.

Someone who knew Russian hastily scrawled on the paper, "We cannot use your money, but won't you bring us milk for our children," and tossed it back to the girl.

She ran off after reading the message, but whether she got milk they never knew, for almost immediately the train moved on again.

Once, as they stopped by a siding, a young girl came staggering towards them crying for help.

She was dishevelled, famished, and covered with lice. It was a Polish exile who had been left behind two days previously from one of the many trains. She had absolutely nothing with her, for all her belongings were with her brother on the train that had left; and she could hardly believe her eyes when a train filled with her own countrymen drew in. And the other exiles, whose belongings were so scanty, felt a sudden gush of confidence in being able to help someone more unfortunate than themselves.

Happily too, soon after she had joined them the train halted at a water tower, and before the guards could possibly stop them many of the children and young people had stripped off their clothes and were playing under the cool shower. It was useless for the guards to scold and threaten that the train would leave: hens clucking at ducklings could not have been more helpless. More and more children scrambled down and ran along the platform to get in the water; this was the greatest lark they had had. The trip for them so far had been chiefly a bore. They had been cooped up for nine days; they had been hungry, uncomfortable, and the older ones were certainly not unmindful of their parents' distress. But it was impossible for them not to consider the whole exodus somehow in the light of adventure. Whether they recognized it or not, a lively curiosity was mixed with their dread of the unknown. And at the first opportunity their high spirits rose and they splashed and shouted with glee.

Their mood infected their elders, for courage is as contagious as fear.

"After all, we carry our means of living with us," said Dr. Zielinski. This was the same man who in Lemberg had protested so vehemently when arrested that his friends feared for his reason. But the calamity had not overwhelmed him: he had regained his composure and Jan now looked adoringly at him again, no longer frightened by that strange father who had shocked him so immeasurably.

"I cannot imagine any Russian town—no matter how important or how small—which will not offer opportunities to a capable general practitioner, or a good lawyer," he went on. "You, my friend"—and he turned to Dr. Altberg—"are lucky in knowing the Russian language; many of the others too, no doubt; but we all of us here are equipped to cope with a new life. *Pani* Kochanska must give concerts . . . we will find her a violin. There must be many Russians who have heard of her and who remember her husband's great reputation. She, too, will find pupils. . . ."

His theme was infectious. It needed but little to rouse *pan* Fischer's optimism, but even Ignac Stupek declared he would open a tailor's shop and rise to the top of his calling. "These Russians understand nothing of fashions. They were always bad dressers, *toujours du mauvais goût*. But let me find a little capital; I'll show them how to make clothes . . . but of an elegance!" He broke off, choked by his own eloquence and the cloud of dust which rose from his clothes when he slapped himself on the chest.

The Rabbi's four sons, fine-looking men ranging from

the age of about eighteen to twenty-six, declared they had no misgivings about the future. "For those who are willing to work—and we are not afraid of hard work—there must be great opportunities. In a land where all is so new and so much remains to be done we shall surely find a place. We can contribute so much."

Each turned his thoughts resolutely from what he once had been and talked only of the new life, dismissing or trying to forget everything that was familiar, beloved, secure. The insane woman drooled and gibbered in her corner, punctuating the discussion with little yelping laughs. As the train jogged on, it shook her inert body and tumbled it into grotesque sprawlings, which her husband strove in vain to check. But although the others did not cease to pity her great affliction, they were no longer appalled at the sight of her: already their compassion was tinged with acceptance. Without knowing it they had relegated her to part of their past life, and her sufferings could not shake their firm faith in what the future held for them.

Late that night the train came to an abrupt halt. Shots rang out and there was a sound of shouting and commotion. It was very dark, but those who pressed their faces to the grating trying to pierce the blackness guessed that they were in no village but still in the midst of woods. Curt orders were given and guards ran along the tracks, banging on the doors of the cars testing locks. Suddenly a rocket streaked the sky, its vivid flame lighting the scene in a shower of gold.

Nothing met the gaze but miles on black miles of straight, bleak trees like burnt matches stuck in rows in the ground.

Excitement gripped the watchers, helpless behind their heavy iron bars.

"It's an escape! Someone has escaped!" The whisper rippled through the train and more and more faces appeared at the gratings. In an instant everyone was secretly wishing the runaway luck in his venture; they watched breathlessly, scanning the woods. It was as if they were all straining to help this daring, unknown creature to evade his would-be captors; all united in the desire to protect him during the man hunt.

Again a flare flooded the sky and three guards plunged into the forest, loaded rifles in their hands.

"Do you think anyone would stand a chance of escaping in country like this?" queried Olga, nervously alert. The idea of flight had never entered her mind before, but now that someone had made the attempt, she found herself stirred by all kinds of crazy speculation.

"The peasants would help you here," whispered Dr. Altberg. "After all, we are not criminals; we are not branded . . . if indeed they still do that to their convicts. One might succeed in mingling with the population of some little village for a while, and later stage a get-away. I should think if anyone could manage to exist for the first two or three days he would be bound to come on some kind of human habitation . . . even here. But whether that would ultimately mean freedom I don't know. Probably not."

They continued to watch and whisper like conspirators. Forgotten were all their plans for the brave new life, gone their resignation. Thought of liberty had suddenly flared . . . like the rocket in the night . . .

snatching their peace of mind and making their hearts beat wildly.

More and more flares were kindled, but after a few hours the guards came back, sweating, exhausted and without their prisoner, and the train moved on. Did he get away, that bold spirit?

Nobody ever knew.

A short time after this adventure a number of passengers were taken off the train and driven away in trucks; nobody knew why, nor indeed if this had any connection with the break-away. The guards refused to talk about it, and there was no opportunity of questioning anyone else, for the travellers noted that the train seldom stopped at the station in the villages, but always half a mile or so beyond. The trucks had been waiting by a siding not far from a junction; but with the exception of their drivers, no one was in sight.

Olga sometimes wondered if the Russians themselves had any plan or knew exactly where they were going. At each halt there was so much discussion with the engine driver, and the same confusion and apparent indecision that had preceded their departure from Lemberg. Some of the passengers had been told they were bound for Kiev; others believed that Moscow was their destination. The train had entered numerous tunnels which everyone supposed ran through the Urals; it had skirted low mountains and spent much of its time in forests, but though the general route seemed to be in the direction of north-northeast, this really indicated very little. "And then, their sense of direction is so faulty anyway!" thought Olga, remembering the Russian Commander of the Lemberg air field, who had come to visit Madame Ostrowska during the early months of occupation. He was describing the Russian campaign in Finland and had pointed to a map of Europe on the wall. "This is where our troops are fighting," he said importantly, placing his finger on the British Isles.

Everyone was getting terribly weary of the long journey. Day succeeded unvaried day and nerves grew more tense and frayed.

"Do you always have to throw cinders all over me?" suddenly snapped Dr. Altberg, as one of the passengers on the upper berth moved abruptly and swept the collected dust to the floor. It was becoming increasingly difficult to maintain good tempers and good manners. The hungry children were never silent: they whimpered or screamed or plaintively begged for something to eat. Even from the adjoining car the newborn baby's wail was penetratingly distinct.

Yet lack of food was easier to bear than the thirst which was an agony night and day. It drove the passengers to desperate lengths and whenever they stopped they swallowed any water they could find, no matter how repulsive. Dysentery plagued nearly everyone in the train, but Mr. Stupek grew seriously ill with it. His temperature ran dangerously high and he rapidly became so weak that some of his companions took turns in standing, in order that he might have room to lie full length in the crowded car.

His fashionable clients would never have recognized this bedraggled creature whose emaciated face was covered with weeks of stubble and whose fine clothes were soiled and black with grime. How he hated himself for the trouble he was causing; how humiliated he felt, his manhood brought so low. Poor *pan* Stupek, all his elegance had vanished! He had intended to face his fate like a hero; to be debonair to the finish, and confound his captors by his gallant behaviour; but his body betrayed him and his jauntiness vanished; his bowels turned to water and he wept with shame.

Another forlorn figure in the car was the youngest Krantz boy, who was nursing a badly cut hand and a broken arm. His sister was still unable to nurse her baby, and the lad had wanted to heat some milk and was trying to make his way into the adjoining car where someone had a primus stove. He had almost forced open the door when guards had seen him and beaten him back, using their rifles so brutally that his hands dripped with blood. But his distress was chiefly for his sister.

"Don't cry, darling," he begged her, while the others, horrified at what they had seen, did their best, with odds and ends of linen, to bind up his wounds. "Little sister, little sister, I'll get something for you yet. Don't worry; don't cry; smile a little." He stroked her cheek and tried to lift the infant from her tired arms, but he winced with pain and could not take the child.

It was late in the afternoon when the train stopped at Sosva, a village on the banks of the Sosva River. All day there had been tantalizing glimpses of water between the dark trunks of pines, making the passengers in the upper berths unusually restless.

So dazzling was the sun along those silver stretches that to the exiles behind their gratings the outside scene was more desirable than ever, a marvellous world of life and liberty fantastic as a fairy tale.

As the train shunted to a siding well beyond the village, they clambered out gratefully and reached the clearing by the river.

"As usual, we seem to stop bang in the midst of nowhere," observed Olga, looking around to see if villagers were approaching the train. She had so hoped she would be able to take her bearings, but her surprise was great when she heard guards informing the passengers that the first part of the journey was over. "You go the rest of the way by boat," they said curtly with no further explanation. And they began unceremoniously dumping everything out of the train which immediately departed as if it had not a moment to lose.

Everyone was dazed at this sudden transformation.

Not a word had been said of any change of itinerary. They had had no opportunity of putting together their possessions which were now scattered all around them in the greatest confusion on the ground.

Yet evidently their arrival had been awaited.

A group of men, with an officer in khaki, stood talking near a woman, in a rough sort of uniform, who was standing by a trestle table serving out thin barley soup and cutting slices of black bread.

"Why, they are going to feed us!" exclaimed Olga. "Can you imagine! After sixteen days they are going to give us something to eat!"

Dragging themselves over to the canteen, the Poles waited to receive their rations. Most of them were so exhausted that they rested on the ground, feebly sipping the first hot food that had passed their lips in so many days. But its effect on their spirits was magical.

The officer made a brief check-up on all the exiles, and a Soviet health inspector began making his rounds, questioning them, taking a few temperatures, making a rough examination of some of the more pressing cases of sickness. There was little he could do in the short time he had at his disposal and considering the great numbers he had to deal with, but his homely remedies helped not a few of the sufferers.

Olga had hoped it would be possible to bathe in the river before the next stage of the journey began. The day was warm and utterly windless, and the water looked very inviting, but when she clambered down the steep bank she discovered the ground was heavy with clay and at the water's edge she began to sink so deeply that she was forced to climb back.

Yet just walking through the coarse grass barefooted gave her exquisite pleasure; the feel of the earth was so comforting after those aching days of travel. To watch clouds move in the sky and the sun's sheen on the water filled her with delight. The pungent scent of pines was like heady wine. She lifted her arms above her head and could have danced with joy.

"You look like a bacchante poised for flight," said a voice beside her.

It was Dr. Altberg. The grim-featured man with the dark rings round his eyes watched her ecstatic movement with a sardonic grin.

Olga blushed and sat down to put on her shoes and stockings.

"I have abandoned all thought of flight," she said ruefully. "But I had set my heart on a swim. Do you imagine we shall get baths when we arrive? I find myself thinking of nothing else."

"I entertain no great hopes for future cleanliness," said Dr. Altberg unamiably. "Nothing I have seen in this country so far leads me to suppose that the inhabitants set great store on washing. But man is an adaptable animal. There is apparently no limit to what he can become accustomed." He moved away, gloomy and pessimistic as always, but Olga refused to be depressed by his mood.

Three steam barges came plying slowly down the river and fetched up by the little wooden jetty. After a tremendous amount of shouting by the bargees and discussion with those on the shore, the boats were made fast and the Poles were hastily divided into three groups and told to go aboard.

Lugging their suitcases they clambered on, and were ordered into the hold.

The barge which Olga occupied had obviously been used for hauling potatoes. Not only was there a prodigious amount of dried earth on the floor, but the peculiarly acrid potato smell was unmistakable.

About two hundred people crowded into the low, dark place, and immediately spread their luggage out for seats as they had done in the train. Dr. Altberg was right about the pliability of the human race. Olga realized how quickly she had learned to fit herself to her surroundings. To have travelled in such a primitive fashion would have seemed impossible to her three weeks before; now like the others, she accepted it almost without comment.

Without comment, that is, until sundown.

With the coming of darkness, a faint buzzing sound made itself heard. A cloud seemed to enter the barge and disappear into the hold. There was a whirring, maddening sound of millions of tiny wings.

The mosquitoes attacked in closed formation.

From the farthest steppes of Siberia they came, these torturing swarms, to gorge themselves on the magnificent meal held captive for their enjoyment. Caught unawares, the Poles struck out, trying to shield their faces, their hands, their ankles. They flapped handkerchiefs, waved newspapers, trying to beat off the insects' furious onslaught. But how long had the little pests been without taste of human blood? In those swampy wastes and vast uninhabited spaces mosquitoes develop a lust for flesh that makes them more feared than wild animals.

"Are we to be eaten alive?" wailed the wife of Rabbi Krantz, this last outrage stinging her into articulate utterance. Her hands feebly flailed at the voracious mass around her head. It seemed as if such horrible fate might be true, for the barges never moved, and the suffocating darkness was stabbed with a million red-hot needles; while over the cries of the tormented the buzzing rose to a paean of triumph.

Each one tackled the problem his own way. Women peeled off their sweaters and blouses, tied them over their heads; they lay down with their faces pressed in the earth on the floor, strove to cover their hands and legs. It was a losing fight, for the hold was so stuffy that they were unable to keep completely covered for long, and the minute they emerged for air the mosquitoes fastened on them.

Olga must have dozed from sheer fatigue, for when she awoke the barge was moving. She could hear the faint chugging of an engine, and water slapped lusciously at the sides. She crouched uncomfortably on the ground, her elbow on a suitcase; though sated with blood, some mosquitoes still sang. At the first streak of dawn she tip-toed out, stepping over the recumbent figures sprawled in such ugly confusion, snoring, breathing uneasily, moaning in their sleep. The picture was grotesque and pitiful, and she wrinkled her nose in disgust. Then in a swift stride she gained the companionway and was out on the foot-wide deck.

A thick mist enveloped the landscape promising heat, but the dawn was chill and still only faintly grey. After the mephitic atmosphere in the hold the pure air was exciting and exhilarating; she drew great drafts into her lungs, hugging herself in the cold. Great shafts of sunshine thrust fingers into the dawnlight. Slowly the mist vanished and the river banks hove into view.

It was a scene of beatific tranquillity.

The broad river wound its slow way through immense pine forests. Not a sound broke the stillness, not a bird, nor the lowing of cattle. At each bend in the wide silver expanse Olga expected some town or village to appear on the banks. But hour after hour the scene never changed: always the same unbroken sweep of pines; not a farm or manor house, no church spire or friendly barn. Here and there a rutted road, ankle-deep in grey dust, wandered into a clearing, leading to nowhere; bald patches loomed, with livid and blackened scars where lightning had struck and giant trunks had crashed down, splintering the small growth; on each forlorn bank a mud belt marked the flood level of the river, and beyond that, in the distance, nothing but pines and ever more pines that stretched to the horizon.

It might have been a landscape on the moon, or something existing before the creation of man. Such solitude was awe-inspiring and somehow very terrible. For three days Olga hardly left her seat in the bows, unable to tear herself from all that emptiness, disregarding even the mosquitoes as she shaded her eyes with her hand, straining into the blue distance.

Late on the afternoon of the third day the barges slackened their speed, and like a breeze through corn ran a whisper that the destination was in sight. The exiles tried to push their way on deck: now that the moment of release was near they could hardly contain their impatience. The long-drawn-out misery of the trip was nearly over; their trials were ended and they could live again.

A broken wooden jetty ran out into the water, now grey with mud churned by the clumsily moving craft. Slowly the barges came to a standstill to allow the passengers to alight. Forgotten were the fatigue and hunger of all the past long days as the exiles made a wild stampede to catch a fleeting glimpse of this, their promised land. The high river banks cut off their view as they landed, but they surged up the sides, breathless to reach the top. Each thought only of himself, intent on that first impression which would reveal the conditions under which they were to live. The old people were left to struggle up alone: Ignac Stupek, still weak and sick with dysentery, slipped and fell in the river, but, shivering with fever and dripping with water, he stumbled out unaided, dragging himself in the direction of the excited, curious crowds.

They stood at the top of the bluff, bewildered at the scene before them.

Here was no town, not even a village to receive them. In a clearing among the trees four lanes of rough log cabins, about two hundred in all, spread out on each side of a stretch of trampled land. A half-ruined sawmill, a few barnlike wooden structures, the blackened skeleton of a burned-out electric-light plant met their gaze.

That was all.

That was their home, the only sign of human habitation in all that bleak landscape.

They could not believe that this was where the Russians intended to bring them. They would not listen to the Commandant, who strode through the encampment, alloting them their huts.

"Here you will live forever."

The bravest broke down at the finality of these words. All their hopes for creating a new life vanished. This was the negation of everything they dreamed. An animal existence, a deliberate frustration and humiliation of human dignity: this was to be their existence.

No pride or courage could sustain them any longer. Even Rabbi Krantz found no words of comfort. Despairingly they flung themselves on the bare boards of the cabins, and all through the night the guards listened to their bitter weeping.

3. PRISON CAMP

Siberia is a name which no Pole ever breathes without a shudder. The very sound stirs memories of tragedy and gloom. The land is accursed, a cemetery of brave souls. How many unconquerable aspirations toward freedom have not languished away amidst the grey grass of the steppes, the mountains and impenetrable forests of these wastes in Central Asia?

Much of this land had riches for the asking: full-flavored fruits, fish and caviar in great abundance, an excellent climate and game so plentiful that Dostoevski writes, "it throws itself on the sportsman's gun. A blessed land," he calls it, "out of which it is only necessary to be able to make profit."

But Russians have always made of it a prison. A succession of czars utilized it only as a weapon of defence against ideas.

After 1831 and 1865, when the urge for Polish independence was stirring and Polish patriots first strove to resuscitate the partitioned state, thousands paid a bitter price for that fight for freedom. Everywhere penal colonies darkened the Siberian landscape; ardent revolutionaries, with irons on their hands and feet, were later joined by doctors, writers, teachers, all in fetters: naturalists, statesmen, university students, and even schoolboys hardly in their teens. The flower of Poland rotted in fetid Russian prisons, their great gifts lost to their own nation, all their high competence ignored and wasted by Russian tyrants.

Again after 1905 the Poles were driven into servitude. Everywhere the tide of social consciousness was rising and all the Czar's prisons could not stem the flood. This time Polish workmen participated in the revolt; in seeking their country's liberty they hoped to find freedom for their class as well.

In vain.

Once more Siberia was their lot. The long convoys wended their desolate way across the continent; in convict trains and on foot, dragging their chains, families torn asunder, perishing by the roadside, the unhappy Poles ultimately disappeared and were forgotten in the grey silence of the steppes.

But for Olga these remote and awful happenings were like something from a legend. Though her father came from Poland, she had been born and raised in Chicago. He was a prosperous physician there, and hers had been the happy sheltered childhood of the average young American. Public schools on the north and south side had been her background; even after her marriage she had spent some years in the Windy City, showing her little son where she had worked and played as a pig-tailed schoolgirl, happy to see him, during those war years and the critical time that followed, growing up with some understanding of all that her country meant to her.

Now, during the first days of her life in a Siberian prison, she was stunned and speechless at the realization of her fate.

To the intolerable ache of her body was added an agony of spirit, haunting racking recollections of bits of family history. No longer stories relegated to the realm of fiction or adventure, but something actual, shockingly true.

Granduncle Kochanski had endured the rigours of a czarist prison.

He had been a priest, a fine pianist; a great patriot. And lived twenty-eight years with manacles on his wrists.

She had often told her boy, with pride, about his father's granduncle.

Jan would sit on her knees for hours, holding her tight, tears filling his great brown eyes with horror at the tale. Jan, who in those far-off Chicago days had held her so tight, to keep her safe from danger. What would he think if he knew where his mother was now?

She brushed her hand abruptly over her eyes. She must not let her mind stray in that direction or she would never find the courage to go on living.

Jan was gone.

She had had no word from Jan since that golden morning—how many months ago?—when he rode away on his great bay mare, with gleaming sabre and clank of spurs, a gallant cavalry officer, to meet the German tanks.

In the distance a gong was sounding.

Prisoners were being lined up for roll call in front of the wooden shack.

The Commandant read the long list of names very slowly, pronouncing them with difficulty and delays. He was the tall, blond young man who had met them at the river and accompanied the convoy until it reached the camp. Evidently he was responsible for the re-education of his charges, for after the roll call he gave them a little lecture concerning their behaviour. They were lazy, dirty bourgeois, he assured them, but the Soviet government was offering them the opportunity to reform their ways. Hard work was to be their salvation; with work they could acquire new virtues. They must all work very hard indeed. . . .

"For those who work, will eat," he promised them, saying nothing of those who were too old or too young to qualify for a meal.

On that bright morning after the first short, dreadful night, the prisoners wandered aimlessly about, inspecting their new quarters, for they had been too stunned and downcast the night before to grasp the details of the camp.

The shack where most had slept was the centre of the community, a clubhouse with chairs and trestle tables made of rough-hewn planks. The cabins, stretching in four long rows, were each divided into two rooms about fifteen feet square, with an old iron or earthenware stove in each section. Wide cracks between the rough floorboards were filled with dried clay that crumbled at the touch. Many of the stoves were cracked or broken and added their quota of rubbish to the thick grey dust which covered everything like a pall. Small windows, smeared and grimy, with many broken panes, rattled in ill-fitting frames from which large gobs of dry clay dropped to the floor. The rooms were wired for electricity, but the plant was destroyed and there were no fixtures anywhere, or bulbs.

Most of the cabins were completely empty. Olga had the impression that they had been in use quite recently; to her, they had a curious air of being "lived in"; but the former occupants must have taken their beds and furniture with them, destroying what they could not cart away, for not a vestige of anything remained.

"Now you must put all this in order, you dirty Poles," shouted the overseer as he assigned them to their respective places, and guards ordered them to begin the work at once.

Each cabin was to accommodate eight persons, four to a room, and Dr. Altberg and his wife begged that Olga might be allowed to live with them. They had spent the long, cruel journey together and had become attached by something more than misery shared in common. Three other families had asked to have her with them too: this tall, slim woman with the eloquent, dark grey eyes made a deep appeal to many of the prisoners. There were few among them who had not, at one time or another, heard her husband perform at concerts. Waclaw Kochanski had been the idol of a music-loving public; and they knew her to be a fine musician as well. Then, of all the hundreds in the camp, she was the only woman to be quite alone; something in her helplessness aroused a general compassion. And though they knew her chances of being released were better than theirs, the fact that she was an American and had been arrested at all was doubly monstrous and made imprisonment twice as hard for her as for them.

She looked hopelessly round the bleak little room which was to be her home for so many weary months.

"How are we going to clean all this?" she asked plaintively.

Other prisoners wondered the same thing too. They needed mops and pails and brooms and dusters, soap and cleaning fluid, wax and paint. And none of these things were to be had. The guards shrugged their shoulders when asked to produce them, and the shelves in the Soviet store were almost bare. Only a few cans of dirty-looking vaseline were on sale—these, and the ubiquitous portraits of Lenin and Stalin, in all sizes and varieties, with life-size busts of both in papier mâché or metal.

So the first morning was spent in the woods, where they all gathered twigs and tried to make brooms out of them, a tricky business for those who have little experience with such things. "And what a waste of time and energy," thought Olga, forgetting that they had all the time in the world, and energy to burn.

Some of the women made brushes out of the tall grass, binding it in bunches with coarse creepers. Olga happened on a bit of rope and teased it out with infinite patience and found she had a mop to sweep the floor.

Everything began to acquire a totally new value in this world where every simple requirement was lacking. It did not seem possible that one could treasure up such old discarded objects, yet she caught herself looking around with new eyes, searching about to see if there were not something, perhaps, which the other campers had left behind. She strayed further and further from the cabins, and under a bush in the forest she discovered a pail, a large tin pail with a handle, but no bottom.

She took it to the store and asked if it could not be mended; an important find like this was surely worthy of consideration!

No one would help her, but next door in the kitchen, someone had put away carefully a scrap of metal, so this was soldered on to the pail and Olga marched off triumphantly, swinging it in her hand.

Now she could get some water!

No one else had any water to wash with.

She had a pail! The first bit of furniture for the house.

Later on, she found a chicken's wing. Just where it came from no one could even guess, for there certainly were not any chickens around. But the wing was there, with fresh feathers on it. Olga pounced on the precious treasure. Just the thing to sweep up some of the all-pervading dust.

Everyone envied her the possession.

"Give it to me," begged one of the cooks.

"No, to me! I want it," shouted the baker.

"It's mine!" said Olga, suddenly fierce and possessive. "I won't let anyone have it." She locked it in her suitcase, preserving it very carefully, for she never found another.

The prisoners still had to sleep, temporarily, in the clubhouse, for cleaning and preparing the cabins was a slow, extensive job. During those hot, short nights some of the men stretched out on the parched ground, lighting fires in a vain endeavour to drive off the swarms of mosquitoes which still kept up their murderous attack.

Inside the clubhouse women and children sprawled uneasily on the floor, and mice came out of their holes and frisked among the strange creatures who had suddenly disturbed their possession of the place.

"If only mice ate mosquitoes," muttered Olga, waking in disgust as the little feet pattered over her face.

She was feeling far from well. After three days' work in the camp her knees and stomach were badly swollen and she suffered so much she was finally unable to get up. Her body was paying the price at last for those rebellious sixteen days in the box car. Dr. Altberg examined her carefully and was sure her kidneys were affected. He advised her to apply to the Soviet dispensary and submit a urine specimen for analysis.

In great pain she lay propped up in a corner of the shack, her coat bundled into a pillow for her head, a shawl thrown over her feet. The Soviet doctor gave her a little medicine, but he threw the specimen away without examining it. He said she might prepare another but added she would probably feel better as soon as she got up to work.

There was nothing to do but get up.

It was necessary to take her place in the queue that waited at the kitchen door for the daily ration of food. Three Polish women had been assigned this arduous job and worked sixteen hours cooking for the entire camp. They had to bring water from a distant well, cut and haul all the wood for the great brick stoves which were always kept lighted under the three iron kettles; they had to scrub the wooden floors, which in spite of all their efforts always were dirty from the clay between the cracks.

Lack of adequate utensils hampered their work; all they had to cook with was a rough stick with which they stirred the only dish they ever prepared, soup made of burnt flour, grits, potatoes or barley.

Each prisoner was allowed a plate of this daily, with a pound of bread, a dark, soggy substance that went through the system like a dose of salts. No one ever knew when the rations would be distributed; it was never two days at the same hour, but word went around the camp when people could line up and get their food. No matter how tired the prisoners were they always had to wait in line. There was never enough of anything to constitute the least surplus; they could never buy supplies for the next day; never enough helpers to relieve them of this burden of waiting around to eat. The only ill humour Olga ever saw was during the hours they wasted daily when someone tried to push ahead and reach the kitchen first.

Once or twice during many months small fish were added to the menu, a kind of pickled herring, much the worse for wear. Why did no one throw a line into the Sosva River? Such unfished waters would surely have yielded a banquet for them all. But prisoners were forbidden to approach the banks, and apparently the gentle art of fishing was one which the Soviet authorities were not anxious to acquire.

Men engaged in really hard labour were, on one or two occasions, sold meat balls, but at almost prohibitive rates. Everything the prisoners ate had to be paid for out of their meagre wages; and even had the fare been much more plentiful or varied, few earned enough to have been able to afford living any better than they did.

Three Russian bookkeepers, sitting in a little room next to the overseers, kept elaborate accounts of each prisoner's work and the amount he was to be paid for it. They looked like little mice scrabbling away with the beads and wires of their abacus, without which they were unable to reckon at all. Rarely did they pay the prisoner exactly what was due him; there were always reasons for making deductions—generally fines for misdeeds committed around the camp or in the fields. A cash sum was paid and credit promised after a given period, at some future date—this latter pretext always involving such intricate calculations and explanations that most prisoners despaired of ever receiving their full due and just took what the bookkeepers handed out.

Five roubles a day was what they were told they would receive, though they rarely got anything like this amount. At a regular exchange the rouble was worth about twenty cents, although its purchasing power was really considerably less. Even simple necessities were exceedingly expensive; a plate of soup was eighty kopeks—almost a rouble!—a pound of bread fifty kopeks; kerosene for lamps was a heavy item in the day's expenses.

Slowly the cabins began to look more habitable. From the abandoned sawmill men had dragged planks and made rough tables and benches: they nailed boards together for trestle beds. All this work was exceedingly difficult to carry out with the broken tools at their disposal; and most of it was done with makeshift methods. There was even a shortage of nails, and these precious objects had first to be drawn out one by one from old timber that had lain around in the rain for heaven knows how many seasons, so the nails were not only bent and blunt but rusty as well. The prisoners worked slowly too, for they were unaccustomed to such heavy tasks.

"You have five thumbs on your hands," grumbled a guard, watching the efforts of a middle-aged man who looked like a professor or scholar.

"You should rather compliment me that I make such good progress," rejoined the spectacled man mildly. "When I came here I could do nothing with my hands. Now I have made myself a bed." He looked with satisfaction at his work. "Isn't that good, *tovarich?*" he added humbly, wishing to placate his tormentor by use of the Russian title.

"Don't call me *tovarich,*" screamed the guard. "That is no term for you to use. I am no 'comrade' to you. Only good and trusty Bolsheviks address each other by that name. You have not reached that level yet. You should say: *grazdanin,* citizen . . . that is all you can claim to be yet; who knows if you will ever be allowed to say *'tovarich'* to me."

He marched off to see what the other workers were doing. The perpetual surveillance was one of the prisoners' greatest hardships. Never was there a moment when they were allowed to be alone. From morning to evening armed guards were standing over them; and that sharpest of all suffering, forced co-habitation, meant that even at night they were denied the consolation of solitude.

Sensitive natures were irked as much by this as by actual chains; they felt as though irons were riveted on their limbs. All of them suffered, particularly during the first summer days of their arrival when the brilliant burning sunshine reacted violently on their nerves, debilitated as they were by long confinement in the gloomy train. There were moments when such constant vigilance was almost unendurable; the tyranny of another's will imposed on their own became more than they could bear.

They did their best to take things lightly, trying to laugh off their irritation and talk about their household preparations. Olga was lucky in having brought with her a sewing reticule, for needles, in this wilderness, were more precious than pearls. She bought a length of coarse cotton material and made herself a mattress —a big bag stuffed with hay was all it was—but with a pillow of the same material and her rug for a cover she was not only more comfortable than she had been for weeks but experienced a singular consolation in the idea of having a bed again, after the long period of bivouacking on the floor.

From the kitchen she managed to buy a small basin, and this, together with her precious pail, equipped the cabin for toilet purposes with a luxury the others could not attain.

It had been an uncomfortable preoccupation for days, this matter of keeping clean. Even after she had rid herself of the hateful vermin collected on the journey, her imagination gave her no peace. The log cabins seemed to offer little guarantee against invasion and she had a fastidious misgiving as to what might not crawl out of the grimy walls. She did her best to freshen the place. With heavy clay from the river banks mixed with water, she helped plaster the entire room, using her bare hands to spread the messy stuff over the walls, patting it smooth, and rejoicing in the resultant pale grey effect when it finally dried and the nauseating odor had disappeared.

The second room in the cabin was occupied by Mr. Fischer, his wife Anna, and the two children Zula and Henryk; while Dr. Altberg and his wife and daughter moved into the front room with Olga. It took no little courage to settle down to this strange intimacy; no little ingenuity too was needed to cope with the living problems.

Every evening they filled the pail with water and next morning took turns at washing and dressing. When Mrs. Fischer began moving about in the next room, calling the children, Olga knew it was time to get up; and when she heard Mr. Fischer doing his exercises, clapping his thighs and arms, it was her turn for the basin—she could ask for the precious object and retire behind the stove for her ablutions. "Only for five minutes, you know, then you must give it back," Mrs. Fischer never failed to remind her every morning.

She was a fretful, ailing woman and inclined to be exigent, even with other people's property, but Olga forgave her, for she knew that the woman had been dragged from a sick bed to be sent on this wild Siberian adventure. Fortunately Mr. Fischer was of a most sanguine disposition, always joking, laughing, soothing his wife's alarms, and really gifted when it came to using his hands. He loved to potter about the house, fixing the beds, sawing wood to make shelves for the walls, devising a latch for the door, and even constructing a small xylophone for their entertainment. This was a little chef d'oeuvre when it was finished, each key carefully planed and drilled and attached to the keyboard by a pin. It made a wonderful accompaniment for their rare concerts, at which Zula would sing like a nightingale. She took after her father, with a lively temperament, which sometimes exploded in outbursts of anger and disobedience. "Little imp," her brother called her, but only in fun, for he was extremely fond of her, even if he did insist that she go in the morning to get the bread for breakfast. "Off you go, Imp," he would call, not stirring from his own bed. "If you don't make haste there will be none left." Which indeed was sometimes the case; and even when she did come back with it she was often crying, for she was a little thing, and got pushed out of line waiting her turn before the store. In spite of her diminutive size she did more than her share of the work, and when one of the guards taunted her with the dirty state of the room, pointing to the ingrained filth which the Poles had 'found on their arrival, she took a piece of tin and went on her knees, scraping and planing for hours, doing her best to make the place look better.

Now that the cabins were finished, everyone wondered what their daily tasks would be.

On the first morning when they had to appear before the *Nachalnik*, the work-giver, there was a great deal of speculation as to what he would demand of them. They all clung to the hope that they could be used according to their professional capacities. They had accepted the hardships of getting the cabins ready, digging latrines, struggling with broken stoves, since there had been no other way of making them habitable; but now that the worst of the preparations were over their hopes began to rise in prospect of an easier time.

"And what do you do for a living?" asked the *Nachalnik*, as Olga's turn came in the long line of applicants.

He looked at her coldly and sarcastically as she stood there in the early morning sunshine.

Her face showed traces of the weeks of hardship and meagre living; the delicate features were more sharply defined; dark shadows under her green-grey eyes made them appear larger than ever. The sun had tanned and roughened her skin whose luminous pallor had been one of her greatest beauties; and grey hairs already streaked the brown curls now drawn back in a meek little knot. She met his eyes with a steady gaze and was not abashed by his loud hectoring tone.

"I am a musician, a violinist," she said. "I want some appropriate work, something which will not ruin my hands for my instrument."

She spoke Russian slowly, but quite fluently and correctly.

"Appropriate!" he shouted, seizing on the word, as if it pricked his conscience. "Appropriate! What is appropriate, I should like to know? All work is appropriate."

The word seemed to infuriate him and he jumped up, pacing back and forth, looking at the group of prisoners as they waited in line, like so many animals expecting to be slaughtered. And he would slaughter them too, bit by bit; and every day a little more; they would be long a-dying, but he would see to it that their death was none the less sure, the dirty Poles!

"So the lady wants something appropriate," he went on more quietly, sitting down again and ruffling a sheaf of papers on the table before him. "Well, you can go into the fields and rake hay. That won't hurt your hands, will it? Not to begin with, anyway. I'll find other work for you later on."

Only too glad to be let off so lightly, Olga joined a group which had been assigned to similar work, and, shepherded by two guards, they all went off in the direction of the fields.

It was a brilliant morning with a rare and invigorating wind blowing through the pines. Though the sun later would be cruelly hot, the early hours had a spicy freshness which made the heart sing; and the sky was a piercing blue.

Beyond the limits of the cabins a vast tract of grassy land ran between the trees. Some of this had already been cut, but several men in Olga's party had been given scythes and told to mow the rest.

They held the rusty implements awkwardly in their hands, uncertain how to begin.

"Like this! You cut grass like this!" said one of the guards, dropping his rifle, and seizing a scythe from one of them. He made a rapid circular movement with it that brought the great blade high over the grass so that not a leaf was touched. He tried again, swinging the scythe with effort and slashing at the coarse grey tufts at his feet. "There!" he exclaimed importantly, handing back the tool. "That's how you do it."

They began painstakingly to follow his example. One lad, it was Henryk Fischer who slept in Olga's cabin, was fairly successful, and though the scythe was obviously much too heavy for him, he used it with beautiful rhythmic movements, sweeping it easily as he turned at the waist, and laying the grass in neat swathes all round him.

"We used to do this exercise at school, in gym," he said with a grin to Olga, panting a little with the effort of lifting the heavy blade. "It's more fun when you really have something to cut."

But the others made small progress, and the guards were voluble in their abuse and continued to shout instructions. The scythes were so blunt that it would have required considerable skill to have got any results with them at all; and the prisoners not only had difficulty handling them but worked in a manner extremely dangerous to everyone who came within striking distance of them.

Olga watched them with faint amusement for some time, then turned to her own job of raking hay. She had a very large wooden rake with two teeth missing.

After she had worked for some time and managed to scrape together a number of very untidy-looking piles, she noticed that three other teeth had fallen out, and went to report to the Russian in charge.

"And I suppose you expect me to mend it?" he asked sarcastically. Nevertheless, that was exactly what he did, for she obviously could not continue using it in the state in which it was.

He took a penknife and cut a bit of pine to begin whittling it down to make pegs. Olga was glad of the opportunity to rest, and as she watched him wondered for the nth time why Russians seem so incompetent.

Any country lad at home could have done the job better and in half the time. In the first place he would have had a real clasp knife with a good blade; he would have whetted it on a stone; and he would have whistled while he worked. Olga remembered with wonder that she had never heard a Russian whistle at any time.

Under the rigorous State control of and interference with every aspect of their daily lives, the people seemed to have lost all joy, and the ability to cope with the hundred and one little problems which present themselves to the average person in the day's round. Since they owned so little they valued nothing. They assumed no responsibility for the care or maintenance of *things*, even expressing a sardonic satisfaction when they broke or went wrong. It was this aloofness, this lack of the customary attachments, which Olga found so disturbing, and which seemed to result in general incompetence.

She thanked the guard when he handed her back the

rake: the new teeth were very wobbly and she felt sure they would soon fall out again.

"But why should I care," she thought; "if they don't give me proper tools, how can I work? And what I don't do today I can do tomorrow. And anyhow, they'll probably let the hay rot here, so what little I do will be so much wasted effort." She was quickly learning the Soviet way, already beginning to reflect what others did, already tainted by the apathy of those about her.

Beyond the fields, deep in the woods, Olga spied red berries on the ground. During the dinner hour she told *pani* Wysocki, the schoolteacher from Cracow, and *pani* Altberg of her discovery.

"They must be wild strawberries," she whispered excitedly. "We could go and pick them; they would taste wonderful with our dry bread."

Such a simple suggestion, and yet how inviting and daring it sounded.

Everyone suffered from the unvaried diet at camp. The watery soup without condiments, the sour bread with no butter or fat of any kind, hardly sufficed to stave off hunger, and left them all with a ravening longing for something good or familiar to eat. Although they had stoves in their rooms now and could have prepared better meals for themselves, they had neither the materials, utensils nor leisure to make more than a little herb tea from time to time. Fruit or vegetables they had simply ceased to believe in.

Stealthily Olga made her plans.

After the morning roll call there was a second check-up of all those at work, and this list of names sent to the commissary department since these, and these only, were entitled to receive rations. But when work was over at five o'clock the prisoners could go to their cabins, mend and wash their clothes, do what they liked; and although guards were never off duty, but snooped around, entering rooms at unexpected moments and generally keeping watch, there was no official checking till the following morning. If someone could vouch for your presence, there was no need to show yourself.

With beating hearts they got ready for the expedition, giggling like schoolgirls as they tied scarves over their heads and faces, provided themselves with gloves and thick stockings, preparing to face the mosquito-infested woods.

They set off in high glee—their first outing alone. How good to set foot on God's own earth without the sensation of a revolver at your back; to pause and watch the streak of a bird's wing against the wide heavens and hear no angry voice urging you on to work; to pick the brilliant flowers, tiny peonies, and aconites; to dawdle, laugh over the bundled, hooded appearance of your companions!

Deeper and deeper they went into the woods, fighting their way through the matted undergrowth. From dark, swampy patches between the trees swarms of insects rose; the sound of their buzzing was audible a long way off. No veils or coverings were proof against their attack: doom-eager, they fastened themselves on noses, eyelids, lips; tiny black gnats seemed to try to penetrate the very pores of the skin.

They were all bitten and stung and came home with swollen, reddened faces, but the fruit was worth it all

—such pungent sharp-scented flavor. The three women crammed their mouths like children, and when they had eaten their fill took home a basket to their friends.

No one had noticed their absence; the expedition had been a complete success.

Emboldened by this, others decided to try their luck another evening, for the weather was good, and now the woods were full of mushrooms.

One by one they slipped out, meeting again beyond the fields and dividing into two groups following divergent paths. Olga and her friends returned home without mishap. But Dr. Zielinski and those with him got into difficulties, sank knee-deep in the treacherous marshes, floundered around, lost their way and were overtaken by sudden darkness.

Back in the cabin Dr. Altberg paced the room in gloomy concern. Kazia, his daughter, had not returned from the mushroom-picking and his habitual pessimism conjured up the direst happenings. In vain his wife and Olga strove to reassure him; as the night dragged on he was miserable and worn with worry.

They dropped off to sleep before dawn, and shortly after five the latch was lifted softly and Kazia came stealing back. She was muddy, drenched to the skin, her face and hands were scratched and bleeding, her stockings torn. She had had a wonderful time.

"When we found we had lost our way, we lit a fire," she explained, hugging her parents, and slipping out of her dirty clothes. "It kept some of the insects off, and afterwards it was really very comforting, for we were quite cold. It's strange how chilly the nights are, after such blazing days. We sat up close together, toast-

ing mushrooms on long sticks and singing Polish songs
. . . very quietly, of course. And then much later the
moon came up, very large and brilliant. It was a wonderful sight, with five or six reflections. It all seemed
so romantic."

She sighed and petted her father and scolded him
for worrying about her, persuading him finally to lie
down again and rest before the day's work began. She
herself did not have to report for work, as she was not
yet sixteen. Yet her days were always very full, for she
had the task of keeping the cabin clean, fetching water,
washing the clothes, trying to press them without an
iron, and mend them with the rapidly diminishing supply of thread and darning wool. She spent long hours,
too, waiting in queues before the store to try to buy
the more exotic articles, like soap or toilet paper.

No notice at all was taken of her escapade, but one
or two of the others were caught by guards as they
crept back to their cabins. True, there was no rule
against picking mushrooms in the woods, but this was
an easy pretext for imposing fines, and the prisoners
were solemnly warned against attempting any further
sorties in the night. They felt they had got off lightly,
and the memory of that adventure was a bright gleam
in the endless procession of grey days.

In punishing the prisoners, the camp authorities
nearly always resorted to fines. Even when these were
not heavy, the formalities connected with their imposition, all the time lost during the examination of "evidence," resulted in a considerable reduction of working hours, and this meant a cut in wages and sometimes
a very real loss of money.

A group of men who had been engaged in cutting down trees in the forest reported late for work one morning. With the primitive living conditions in the cabins this was not to be wondered at, but the overseer chose to regard it as sabotage. The men, he declared, were shirking their responsibilities and must be punished; but instead of condemning them himself, he ordered them to appear before a court in a village some sixty miles away.

Under an armed escort they set off to cover the distance on foot. At first they were inclined to regard the outing as a diversion. Getting away from the camp broke the monotony of their days, and the prospect of the long march did not appall them. But through the thick undergrowth they could make but very slow progress. They had to thread their way through a dense forest of birch, aspen and pine; they plodded for miles over prairies where the treacherous carpet of long interwoven grasses hid marshes in which they sank, sometimes to their waist.

The guards, forced to endure the same calamities as their captives, and none too pleased about it, made no effort to hurry.

"The slower you go the further you get," they quoted listlessly; and it took them all of five days each way to accomplish the trip, bivouacking at night as best they could.

The court fined the Poles a few roubles for being late on their jobs, but when they finally got back to camp they had missed ten days' work and forfeited a third of a month's wages, quite a serious matter. In addition to all the exertion and stress of the trip, they went short of food for the rest of the month. Yet the overseer insisted that they had been treated extremely leniently, as the fine had been a minimum one; and the maddening lack of logic in his bland refusal to recognize the fact that they had been heavily penalized merely increased the prisoners' resentment.

The Bolsheviks rationalized everything they did. The indignities and brutalities they practised were invariably accompanied by a façade of formal justification.

A commission consisting of two doctors arrived at the camp to examine everyone and qualify them for work, grading them according to their capacity to do hard, medium, or light. The medical examination was conducted with the utmost solemnity, and for several days the prisoners entertained hopes that their miseries were at an end, for in many cases their obvious physical disabilities should have spared them the tasks which they had been forced to undertake.

Two girls had felt particularly aggrieved by their treatment on this score. They were sisters, no longer young, one a practising lawyer, and the other a pianist of some repute. Their health had become very bad in camp; they were plagued with boils and both had goitre. The doctors passed them for light work, but when the commission had departed the girls were sent into the forest to saw and stack wood.

"But we were qualified for light work!" they protested.

"Quite right," answered the *Nachalnik*. "This is light work."

"In that case, what do you consider hard?" they demanded.

But the *Nachalnik* did not deign to reply, and in spite of all their protestations and tears, they were kept at this job for weeks.

There was no appeal against the camp leaders' arbitrary decisions. The prisoners knew that they were at the mercy of the men who held them. No higher court would ever hear their complaints; the outside world would never know their plight. This knowledge wore them down; there were times when they were overwhelmed by the flagrant injustice done them; yet, did they make an effort to resist, the Russians never failed to prove that they, the prisoners, were in the wrong.

The mother of one of the younger children refused to report for work. She declared that she was ill and could not stand the strain of such hard labour. She was immediately arrested and spent several days in a gaol— a cabin with iron bars. Another woman was punished in a similar manner because she had wandered away from her appointed task one day and spent her time idling in the woods.

Both women were released only when they had signed an official declaration, duly attested and, no doubt, deposited in the camp archives. The former confessed that she had only simulated illness and that she really enjoyed the best of health; and the latter that she had strayed away in order to visit another camp for the purpose of speculation!

But not every prisoner was lucky enough to get off with a faked statement.

The four sons of Rabbi Krantz were ordered to report for work at Lejkin, a prison camp some ninety miles away.

As work slackened at one penal colony, the prisoners were shifted to others: there had already been a certain amount of interchange, and news had seeped back concerning life in the Lejkin barracks. It was a grim, terrible place. Men and women in groups of thirty and forty slept together in vermin-infested shacks; the food was bad and the work extremely strenuous. The Rabbi's boys were required for canal digging, this in spite of the fact of the fact that the first frosts were setting in and the youngest still had his arm in a sling.

From the very first the Russians had looked askance at the venerable Rabbi. They would not forbid his conducting prayers in his cabin, but they refused to allow other prisoners to participate in the ceremonies.

"Such meetings are not politically sound," was their argument.

"Such meetings are not political at all," replied Rabbi Krantz tranquilly. He was a force in the camp, a source of moral fortitude; but the Commandant was far too wily to discriminate against him. He was an old man, a feeble man; he had an old wife, a feeble wife; his daughter was a sick woman, she had a two-months-old child to nourish. The case was an easy one to deal with.

"Send the four sons to Lejkin," ordered the Commandant.

The boys received the orders with a dogged expression.

"And what about wages?" they asked.

There was no information on this point.

"But we must have some assurance that we shall get enough to be able to live there, and still be able to send some back here," they pleaded.

"My sister cannot work, she is sick and has her baby to look after; I must help take care of her," said the youngest boy, hiding his broken arm as he pushed forward to argue with the soldiers. "Someone has to pay for the rations here, we must make enough for all."

So much discussion was unwonted; the guards were becoming restive, and began bawling abuse at the top of their voices. The lads redoubled their opposition.

People came running out of their cabins to see what was the matter. It was the dinner hour, and they were frightened by the sudden commotion on the campus.

"But no, but no, we cannot leave like this. We must come to some arrangement first. We are not afraid of hard work, but we cannot leave old and defenceless people without knowing how they can be provided for."

The lads' voices rose together in a shout and more guards came running up; Rabbi Krantz joined the scene, wringing his hands and adding his protests to the turmoil, and in an instant the Commandant could be seen hurriedly coming towards them, his hand on his revolver.

"What's all this noise about?" he demanded curtly. "I ordered these men to leave for Lejkin. Why haven't they started?"

"We only want to be assured about wages . . ." began one of the boys.

His father interrupted him, turning imploringly to the Commandant. "They can't . . . they can't leave us," he protested. "They are all we have. . . ." He laid his hand for an instant on the other's arm.

Steputin drew his revolver from its holster, firing

wildly into the air, then turned on the old man and felled him with a blow in the face. He kicked the prostrate form contemptuously aside and strode over to the four men, one of whom was trying to raise his father in his arms.

"You will leave immediately . . . but immediately," he shouted.

He made a sign to one of the guards, who dragged the lad from his father and forced him to his feet. Swinging their rifles the guards closed in around the four, and used the butt ends to drive them from the scene.

Sudden silence gripped all those who watched.

Down the lane between the log cabins marched the four young men . . . nothing in their hands, not even an overcoat on their backs.

The camp never saw them again.

4. CAMP PERSONALITIES

Zimny Gorodok was the name of the camp; it was just a speck on the Sosva River, a left-hand tributary of the mighty waters of the Ob, which empties itself in the Arctic Ocean. "Little cold town" is what the name means in the dialect of the district, and Olga remembered the long Siberian winter and shuddered to think what the words implied.

But now the weather was mercifully fine and dry. Although early mornings and evenings were crisper than when they had first arrived, the daytime was hot and sunny; and the nights still incredibly short. When she got up to dress, the sky was flushed and rose-colored; its shimmering opalescent beauty a poignant contrast to the drab squalor of the camp. Every evening brought sunsets of burning glory; such a piling-up of crimson and purple and gold-flooded clouds that Olga stood rapt and awed before the flaming heavens. Never had she seen such massing of savage color, nor breathed such keen, pine-scented air. It put new heart into everyone. No matter how despondent the prisoners might feel, it was impossible not to respond in some measure to the pure, invigorating atmosphere, or to take hope again at the sight of the sky's triumphant splendour.

Slowly they bent their backs to the stern routine of their prison life. Olga's work became increasingly harder; the overseer seemed to delight in imposing unwelcome tasks.

"And how is the musician today?" he asked her, with mock solicitude, making his unfailing rounds and finding her hoeing a field of potatoes. She had to use all her strength to force the hoe's blunt edge into the hard, caked earth; yet much of her effort was wasted, for the handle wobbled unsteadily with every movement. There was a nail missing and it was badly bent, making her work both difficult and needlessly tiring. Her back ached, her hands were calloused and bruised. She paid no attention to the man's remarks as he strutted before her, an absurd, unpleasant figure in his green and red shirt.

His name was Holin, but they called him *Jaskrawy* behind his back, the "gaudy one," and laughed at his execrable taste in clothes. They knew he hated to be shown indifference, for he really thought himself quite a fine fellow, so they ignored him as much as possible and paid no attention to his sneers.

"Do you think you could play a violin now . . . if you had one?" he went on, trying to arouse her anger. She said nothing but spread out her hands, with their broken and bleeding nails, before him. "Not that I have any intention of letting you get hold of one," he added, piqued by her silence and her gesture, and strolled off towards the others.

Olga set her teeth and finished her hoeing.

She had another hateful job before her, sorting the potatoes she had hoed. This meant plunging her hands among the earth-covered mounds. She must throw out all the rotten ones, then divide the big from the small and carry them all to the store. She was appalled at the numbers that had been allowed to freeze and rot. Such waste again, though she was sure that half the potatoes cooked in the kitchen were bad.

She had worked for days sorting potatoes in one of the barges that put in at the jetty. Thousands of pounds had been lost between the camp and the place where they started from, Schaborow, only a few miles away. Just what had happened to them nobody knew. Some were stolen, no doubt; some went rotten and had to be thrown out; some were "mislaid." An overseer had already been dismissed for his carelessness, for he had been responsible for part of the loss; he had piled the barge so full and let it stand so long that in the dark warmth the potatoes had begun to shoot. Olga never forgot the stench of those sprouting tubers. But what was the loss of one overseer? Another overseer took his place—and the potatoes that had been saved were left out at night to freeze. The next overseer threw ashes over them. It was all the same to him if the piles diminished too rapidly. Someone would eat less potatoes, that was all. But the overseer would certainly not go short.

Best of all, Olga liked working in the forest, far away from the odours and tedium of the camp. She was sent there to pick whortleberries one day, together with Maria Wysocki, who lived near her log cabin.

They worked silently and conscientiously for many hours, slowly filling their boxes with fruit. Then Maria straightened her back and put down her load.

"There! Now we've picked enough, let's sit down and talk," she said.

She was a fine-looking woman of about forty, a schoolteacher and graduate of the University of Cracow. Even the guards were a little impressed by her presence, and she treated them with good-natured tolerance, as though they were part naughty little boys and part intelligent students.

"You can't stop now, you know," objected the guard at once when he saw her sitting down. "You must get on with your work."

She laughed easily, drawing a little packet of tobacco out of her pocket.

"Ah! Work . . . work!" she exclaimed, her voice plangent, cajoling yet full of authority. "Work isn't a bear, it won't run off into the forest." He smiled at her use of the old Russian idiom and she smiled back, then turned on him commandingly. "A strong man like you," she scolded, "to do nothing but stand with a revolver over two weak women who work! Aren't you ashamed! Go and look after your other prisoners." He shifted uneasily under her eagle eye, but she continued to stare at him fixedly, so he shuffled off and began giving orders to another prisoner not far away.

Maria sank back in the grass and began filling an incredibly crumpled bit of paper with tobacco. There was almost no paper at all in camp and even the dirtiest fragments were cherished for rolling cigarettes. *Mohorka*, that strong, evil-smelling weed Russian peasants smoke, was occasionally sold at the Soviet store, and in spite of its rank flavour Maria sighed with satisfaction as she drew a few puffs, inhaling luxuriously and watching the smoke curl up faint and blue in the warm still air.

"*Ah* . . . that's good," she said, at last. "You should smoke, Olga Kochanska, it makes one's heart glad. And not to be glad at something is to be already dead."

"Do you find so much to be glad for, here?" asked Olga sadly, dispersing the wreaths of smoke with her hand.

"One must learn to look for new joys," said the other woman, her deep voice so vibrant with pain and passion that Olga was startled at its quality. "Today one finds them in strange places and under strange circumstances. My sister in Warsaw told me that she found a new reason for thankfulness . . . emerging from the dank gloom of a cellar when the 'all-clear' sirens sound. To come out into the sunshine and know you are alive —that is something to be glad for!"

She continued to smoke in silence for some time, but the pause was full of friendly understanding.

"I'm glad I brought my little baby with me too, here to this awful camp," she went on. "Such a tiny thing . . . my friends urged me to leave him behind, but wouldn't I be worrying all the time now, not knowing where he was or what was happening to him? No, I did right to bring him and I'm glad of it. Now I'm not alone. I have someone to care for. It was bad luck, of course, that I ever left Cracow for his birth, but I'd had a bad time waiting for him. I'm old, you know, to be having my first baby. My husband thought I would get better medical care in Lemberg . . . and then war broke out and I couldn't get back. But maybe I would have been arrested in Cracow anyhow. I've had no word at all from Taddeus, so they have probably arrested him too. He is a much finer teacher than I am, and it's education that these Russians fear most and are trying to destroy. An enlightened mind, capable of independent thought . . . ah! most dangerous . . . most dangerous," and she shook her head in comical dismay.

"You are very brave to think the way you do, and to try to be glad for so little," said Olga admiringly; "I only wish I had half your courage."

"Why, Olga Kochanska! You are one of the things I am glad for most."

"I am?" repeated Olga in great astonishment.

"You hold your head so high, and you walk so straight," replied Maria, smiling. "You look so . . . so undaunted. I like to watch you move . . . it makes me think of a flight of birds . . . or arrows . . . I don't know . . . something winged and clean-cut. Has no one ever told you that before?"

Olga was silent a moment. "I have not thought of this for years," she said at last, speaking very slowly. "But your words remind me of something Waclaw said . . . about life being meaningless except in motion. It was one winter evening . . . we were skating. . . ." Her voice broke suddenly, for she never mentioned Waclaw to anyone in camp. But Maria patted her hand and nudged her shoulder encouragingly. "I used to go and meet him on the canal, and once, at some quick, skimming movement . . . it must have been the wind in my skirt, or the sudden gleam of skates in the dark . . . he said it was like a swift musical phrase. . . ."

They sat in silence a while, each deep in her thoughts, then quietly rose and continued picking berries.

It was rare that Olga lifted the heavy folds of her reserve, and now she felt refreshed at this unburdening of memories. In the log cabin that was her home she never talked about herself or her family with the Altbergs.

Though they showed her nothing but kindness, life was conducted with the politest formality, strangely at variance with their promiscuity. "*Pani* Kochanska," they always said, never using her first name; "*pani* Altberg," she always answered, never omitting the title. Unconsciously, perhaps, they clung to their former social distinctions, lingering over a detail of what once had been, in a pathetic attempt to preserve some elegance of address amid the brutal circumstances of their surroundings. Perhaps, too, they did it in defiance of the Russians, who expressly forbade all titles.

"Here there is no *pan*, no *pani*," said the Commandant coldly, when first the prisoners arrived in camp. He wished to make it very clear from the start that there would be no respecting of position and persons.

How they hated him, that tall, blond man who was the master of their fate. His name was Steputin, but they always referred to him as *Ponuri*, literally "sourpuss," for never were his stern, coarse features seen to relax in a smile. He was about twenty-six, a perfect product of the Soviet system, for he was too young to have known or remembered any other form of government. Though the prisoners did not feel he was actually unfair, and only on one occasion did Olga witness an act of brutality on his part, his cynical indifference to human feelings amounted almost to an organic defect. Nothing moved him; he showed an animal insensitivity to suffering; he was cold, suspicious and terrible too, for he possessed absolute power over six hundred human beings.

Their simplest requests he vetoed, or, if he granted them at first, he immediately withdrew his consent as though to prove his power. Old Mrs. Krantz begged him to let her use her primus stove in her cabin. Cooking was so difficult in the big brick stove, it was more then her feeble hands could manage, and she wanted to prepare the boys a cup of herb tea before they went to work. He let her do it once, twice, then sternly forbade it and confiscated the primus. Workers in the fields asked permission to roast a few potatoes as they worked. Even the poorest peasants in Poland enjoyed this privilege; he not only refused but warned the guards to be on the lookout lest anyone disobey.

Forever spying on his victims, once he came into Olga's room, pushing the door noiselessly, and surprised her while she was dusting with her precious chicken's feathers. She wheeled around, her right hand extended, a gracious figure of a hostess, welcoming a long-awaited guest.

"Ah, *Pan* Steputin!" she exclaimed dramatically, her mocking eyes dancing over his awkward figure. He backed out of the cabin, uneasy, abashed, unable to rise to the occasion and respond to her irony.

He lived in one of the bigger buildings near the club-house, but although he had two rooms for himself and his wife, when she finally arrived, these were furnished in the simplest manner, and his food was cooked in the common kitchen.

Gossip said that this was his second venture in matrimony, this big-boned blonde who strode through the camp swinging her arms like a soldier. She was only eighteen years old, almost as tall as her husband, with coarse features and stringy hair, though not exactly ugly. Had she spent a little time on herself, worn attractive clothes, she might have passed as good looking, but she either did not care enough or know enough to make the best of her looks. Her big-hipped body in its shabby sweater showed only too clearly that she wore no girdle; a full serge skirt flapped about her ankles; her shapeless, nondescript coat was topped by a shawl-like collar of mangy fur that mounted untidily into her hair behind and made her seem hump-backed.

They said she had been a schoolteacher, but what studies had she done, asked the Poles, and where could she have obtained diplomas when she was only eighteen now? She did not teach school at camp, but occasionally worked in the dispensary, handing out remedies in an automatic fashion, hardly listening to her clients, a sullen, unfriendly figure.

Did this impassive pair ever show any warmth of feeling even when alone? the prisoners often wondered. All their normal impulses seemed suppressed. Or was their attitude the result of Bolshevik education, in which private lives and interests were sacrificed to those of the State? Was the Soviet aim a deliberate cult of heartlessness, lest conflicting loyalties weaken their stranglehold on the people? So it seemed to the.prisoners, watching Steputin and his wife. Not only did their behaviour bear out the theory, but their attempts at educating the young people in camp appeared to confirm this too.

There were about forty children between the ages of six and sixteen at Zimny Gorodok. Apart from the housework around the cabins there was nothing to fill their days. Their lot was pretty dreary, for their parents were at work from morning till night; and although none of the children believed that the camp life was anything more than a horrible interlude, and that one day they would all be free, time hung very heavy on their hands. They were always hungry and none of them slept enough on their plank beds during the short light nights. The very old people had all they could do in looking after the infants and could give no attention to these adolescents, so Steputin decided to start morning school.

The first teacher came from a nearby town, some two hundred miles away, and the children took to her instantly. Tatiana was her name, a sweet-faced, smiling girl with the softest, sweetest voice. She sang to the children and taught them Russian songs, and showed such a friendly interest in them that they loved her, and an atmosphere of confidence was established at once.

For the first time children's laughter rang through the camp; they went to school with glee.

Steputin immediately changed all this. Tatiana was dismissed and another teacher took her place—a much older woman, with a grim, worn face, who brought her husband with her and a cow.

The man looked like a shepherd; and the Poles were shocked that anyone in a liberal profession could ally herself with such a ragged, dirty creature. That was decidedly lowering the educational status, they thought.

There was no more singing and laughter; but daily lessons in Bolshevik history, arithmetic, Russian. The teacher was very dull, and the work so elementary that many of the older boys and girls stopped attending classes, finding it a waste of time.

The cow was considered a great acquisition, and at first seemed likely to make the teacher popular. Milk, however, was such a precious commodity that she could afford to behave in the most capricious manner about selling it and quickly lost everyone's esteem.

When in winter Dr. Altberg fell ill, Olga hurried to the woman, begging her for milk and was graciously allowed to buy a quart for five roubles—more than a whole day's wages. The Altbergs could ill afford this sum, but the man was very sick and they managed to scrape it together. Next time, however, the teacher declared that she could not sell them milk for money alone; they must give her sugar as well, for she knew they still had a small supply of this from what they brought with them from Poland. This was a great blow, for it was practically impossible to buy sugar in the store and they knew they could never replace it; however, they dug into their hidden treasure to get the coveted milk; but even this did not satisfy the woman for long. The third time Olga went she refused to sell her anything at all—she had found a more advantageous market, so the sick man went back to the dirty lumps of frozen milk which peasants sometimes brought into camp for sale.

Of all the inmates of Zimny Gorodok, only two were able to defy the authorities and seemed unmoved by everything around them.

Icek and Lejba were young Jews in their middle twenties, who had been arrested in Lemberg, though their home town was Jaroslaw. There they had enjoyed a carefree independent existence, vaguely connected with the movie world; though just exactly what they did no one knew precisely, for both men were more than a little unbalanced when they arrived, and the camp's hardships apparently aggravated their crazy behaviour.

Icek, the younger, was a fair, handsome fellow, though many of the prisoners were frightened by his unkempt appearance and rolling eyes in whose dark blue depths something frantic lurked. He never stopped talking and ambled about the camp, admonishing guards, giving them advice, refusing to work.

"Why do you work?" he demanded of everyone he saw. "What are you working for?" His voice went echoing through the camp. "You, *pani* Kochanska, you shouldn't work. You don't have to work. You are an American, why should you work for Russians?"

Olga was engaged in carrying water from the well, walking very slowly and carefully, for it was a long distance from the camp up a steep hill, balancing the heavy buckets with difficulty, anxious not to spill the water and get wet. He followed her back and forth, offering once to carry a pail, but he was so dirty and wild-looking, and smelt so bad she did not want him near her and would not accept his aid. But nothing would stop his chatter and she marvelled that the Bolsheviks accepted as madness all he said and did. At times, she thought he had more sense than anyone in camp.

"We needn't work," he asserted. "We'll be going back to Poland soon. We don't have to work for Russians." No one but Icek dared to utter such heresies. "General Sikorski is still fighting . . . we'll have a country soon. I'll see you and hear you in Warsaw, *pani* Kochanska, before long. Why do you work? You were so pretty once, but now you've changed. You shouldn't work . . . you really shouldn't work."

Strangely enough, he and his brother were the only males of working age in all the camp who did nothing and yet did not suffer and go hungry. They marched boldly to the commissary, demanding food, and something in their crack-brained rantings must have touched a fellow creature, for they were never sent away empty-handed from the door.

Holy Russia had long since ceased to be, but doubtless there were those who still cherished remnants of the ancient Slav belief that madness is akin to holiness; and that divinity, in any guise, must be acknowledged. Icek approached the Commandant too, ambling and babbling, the only one in all the camp who did not fear the morose Steputin.

"Look at me," he would say, "look at my clothes.

Have you ever seen such rags?" Nobody certainly went around in such a destitute state. His coat was almost falling off him and was tied together with bits of rope and string. His pants were torn in such large rents and in so many places his private parts were exposed. "Look at me! Give me a suit," he demanded of Steputin, "I need a new suit."

Someone covered his nakedness, though nobody credited Steputin with the deed. Yet Icek hardly seemed aware he was clothed and shuffled off unconcerned and jabbering.

His brother was more moody and sat mumbling to himself. "It's those eyeballs that did it," he always maintained. He had some terrible complex about eyeballs; they followed him wherever he went, and were responsible for all his woes. "Look at those eyeballs. It's all on account of those eyeballs! If only it weren't for those eyeballs!" he whimpered.

Then he would remain very quiet, hugging and clutching at himself as if he were cold or afraid. But sometimes he forgot his fears and lay back in the sun, singing old Hebrew songs. He had a beautiful voice, and even Olga overcame her repugnance for the pair and crept up to listen to the low, deep-toned melodies that poured out with such aching sweetness; songs of ancient captivity endured by other Jews under foreign skies.

Both lads were worried about their old mother, who had been left behind when they were arrested. They seemed even less crazy than ever when they talked about her; and their anxiety did not differ greatly from that of any other camp inhabitant who had been carried off, unwarned and unprepared, with no opportunity to make provisions for those who were dependent on him.

"In Poland we had everything," cried Icek one day, as though he had only now become aware of his present plight. "Why don't we have things here?"

He may have been mad, as the Russians insisted he was, but his wail echoed all that the other prisoners thought: "At home we had everything."

Only occasionally did they grumble and break down, those indomitable exiles, when over-work had weakened their resistance and frayed nerves snapped; but they did their best to check the sudden bursts of weeping with courageous resolution. Yet they could not help *thinking* of the past; they liked to talk together, particularly the women, of that fabulous "once upon a time" which had been their life in Poland.

Old Mrs. Spiro was eighty-two, erect and white-haired, with eyes that snapped and crackled with a wintry flame. Her son shared her log cabin, a handsome man of sixty with iron-grey hair and his mother's splendid dark eyes. They originally came from Rzeszow, near Cracow, but for thirty-six years he had been a prosperous New York business man, who only, by the merest chance, was visiting Poland when the war broke out.

"Harry had just bought me a really beautiful home in Lemberg," Mrs. Spiro loved to tell her neighbours; "we had hardly settled in when the events happened." She scorned the use of any more ruthless term in describing their arrest. "My unmarried daughter was living with me; she indulges in prolonged ill-health; liver, you know, always a distressing malady." At this point the little old lady could never resist preening herself on her own admirable constitution. "Harry was on the very point of returning to America when the events overtook him."

"Tough luck," he used to say to Olga, stroking his little goatee beard, and twinkling at her with eyes that always tried to smile. "I miss my New York barber . . . chap who always came to look after me at the hotel where I stayed. . . . I wish I could get back to him. But *you're* all right, you are sure to get out," he always assured her. "You've a ninety-nine per cent chance of getting away and returning to the U. S. A. Mark my words, now."

More than his words was his reassuring presence, his handsome appearance and well-kept clothes. Olga would never have believed what comfort there could be in the well-marked creases of a pair of grey-striped trousers. She and he would talk together of life in American cities, of American ways, and American food.

The guards had taken thirty thousand roubles off him before he left Lemberg, but evidently his finances were not exhausted, for he was able to provide for the two women dependent on him although he was too old to work in camp and draw his rations. Olga knew he worried at times about the future, but he never dropped his gallant bearing. "A ninety-nine per cent chance," he always called to her whenever he saw her.

Irena Hind was a pretty elegant woman, whose husband, a Pole of English descent, was a wealthy engineer of Katowicz. "When I think of our apartment there, the warmth and comfort, I get desperate," she once confided to Olga. "If no help comes to us here, and we have to remain another year, I shall make a break for it to try and escape, or else drown myself. I cannot stand this life." She had spent a long day stacking wood under the orders of a particularly unpleasant guard, and she was near the end of her forces. The Hinds, too, were constantly anxious about the fate of their children, a boy of eleven and a thirteen-year-old girl, who had been in the mountains near Zakopane with their nurse when their parents had been arrested, and from whom they had had no word.

It was always those who feared for others who suffered most. To support the hardships of the camp was something one could steel oneself to bear, but the agony of wondering what had happened to one's loved ones—not even knowing if they were still alive, and sometimes almost praying that death had spared a thousand imagined horrors—that was a form of mental torture that made the strongest quail.

Yet the spectacle of children's sufferings before one's eyes was also not an easy thing to bear.

Mrs. Kowalski lived in a cabin with her two daughters and a seventeen-year-old son. They were a cultivated Catholic family, doing their best to adjust themselves to the strenuous Siberian life.

The boy was put to draught work, hauling planks and heavy timber in the half-deserted sawmill. He ruptured himself lifting loads beyond his strength, and his mother appealed to the camp doctor for a belt or medical bandage to wear when he was at work. That doctor was a *feldsher*, the prisoners declared, a man who should have been better employed looking after curs.

"Take your sheet, woman," he told her; "you can tear that into strips and make a bandage." Her only sheet, the single object she possessed that made her think she had a bed to lie on!

One of the boy's sisters took on his task while he rested at home a short time, but the work was far too strenuous for her and brought on a violent hemorrhage. Her mother was at her wit's end with two of her children prostrate, though the doctor treated it all lightly enough and could hardly be persuaded to attend the girl. It was a fortnight before she could stand again, and for months she dragged herself around, unable to work at all. Then she had to return to the forced labor again, but her frail health could not stand it. This time the hemorrhage was so severe that her life was despaired of.

Only one prisoner in the camp received charity from the authorities; this was Mrs. Levi, an elderly Jewess, a fragile creature of seventy who seemed utterly bewildered to find herself alone in such a milieu. She was far too old and weak to work, she who before had hardly dressed herself unaided, who all her life had been dependent on her children, friends and servants. Now, solitary, bereft of every attention, she tottered about, a piteous figure, growing each day more ragged and neglected, more fixed in her belief that she was a sane woman living in a world of raving lunatics. Nothing could persuade her that the Bolsheviks were not, every one of them, as mad as hatters. "Else, why live as they do?" she argued feebly.

Words failed her when she gazed on the filth and primitive lack of decency surrounding her. "With wealth within their grasp, and they choose such penury!" she exclaimed disdainfully. She lifted haughty eyebrows in mute condemnation of the régime, waiting to be rescued, like the occupant of some luxurious automobile stalled in a slum.

She accepted her daily dole of bread, nibbling it daintily, dazed, unable to cope with life and all its perplexities, talking vaguely of a wealthy son in America who might come to her aid if the madmen all about her would only send him word.

"He lives in Omaha, Nebraska; do you know the place?" she asked of practically everyone she saw. "Omaha . . . Omaha . . ." she kept repeating, as though the name would work a miracle, there, in the depths of Siberia.

Olga was working on one of the deserted cabins salvaging building material. The Soviet authorities were going to construct a bathhouse, so she was set to pulling bricks out of broken stoves; sorting whole bits of wood from rotting window frames; collecting nails, which she would later have to hammer and straighten. Nothing could have been more painful for the hands, nor more distasteful; but it was a golden, tingling morning after three days of frigid drizzle, and as she worked she hummed a little tune under her breath.

"That's the Wieniawski concerto you're singing, isn't it?" observed the guard softly, speaking to her in Polish.

She started with surprise, not only because he recognized the melody, but because he spoke her tongue.

She looked at him closely: he was not armed and his face seemed familiar.

"How is it you speak Polish?" she asked. She could not bring herself to mention music: that was a realm in which only friends could meet and she would not share it with those who had brought her to this baleful region.

"I am Polish," he replied. "I came with you in the convoy from Lemberg. The Russians are using some of us on guard duty: they call us brigadiers, and put us on our honour to report about your work. There are too many of us here for the Bolshies to watch as closely as they would like to all the time; so a few Poles are taking over . . . one to every brigade of ten prisoners, and a Russian over us all. I report to Kurkof . . . you know, *pan* Kurkof!" He grinned, and Olga smiled too at his reference to the skimpy little fellow with the pock-marked face who was so flattered when his charges ironically gave him this title.

"He's not a bad chap, quite simple, and doesn't really know how he ought to treat us all," went on the brigadier. "For a long time he believed what the Commandant told him about our coming here because we admired Russia so much and preferred it to living in Poland. Can you imagine believing such talk? Now he's begun to think that maybe that story isn't true, and he's bewildered." The man laughed and began whistling softly. "Don't you love the Chopin Nocturnes transcribed for violin? . . . Ah! If I only had my fiddle here!" He sighed.

"Do you play much?" asked Olga, sitting down on the step of the cabin and letting her hands fall idly in her lap.

"I shouldn't even speak of playing, to you," said the

brigadier, half apologetically. "I don't do much myself, though there isn't a concerto I'm not familiar with. They keep running through my head as I stand around now . . . it's all so futile here. I like to think of them while I'm on guard."

They talked of music, of what they liked most, of how they played this, and that; then he turned away and began to whistle again with a full, fluting tone, staring out between the clearing before the cabins, out and beyond the desert space to where a faint blue ridge rose on the immensely distant horizon. Olga sat leaning her head against the side of the door, staring into the distance too.

The guard's words, and above all the music, transported her to another world, a world of beauty and harmony in which the order was of an inner compulsion appropriate to the form, not clamped on from without by ruthless brute coercion. A world where men and women neither spied upon each other with sharp suspicion, nor were debased by misery to a level where they ceased to regard each other at all.

The brigadier looked carefully in each direction from the cabin. "You sit here and take it easy," he told her, under his breath. "I'll go and see what the others are up to." He walked off slowly in the direction of the other abandoned cabins, and she continued to rest, sitting in the comforting sunshine.

She had found a friend. There was no mistaking the warmth and understanding in the guard who whistled Chopin and who thought Debussy's quintette one of life's major joys. And it would certainly make a difference to the day's assignment to have an overseer who did not always threaten with his revolver and hound you on to work.

It was a satisfaction to know that he could appreciate too how hateful any job becomes once it is obligatory. Hard labour is hard not merely on account of the effort it entails, but because someone has the power to make you do it.

She hoped he would often be on duty when she worked, though even he was subject to surveillance. For the Bolsheviks did not overlook the fact that Polish guards might well close their eyes to lack of Polish diligence.

In the potato fields one morning the baker's son suggested that all the workers form themselves in two contingents, each competing against the other to see who could accomplish the most work. "The winners will be called the Stakhanovite contingent," he said beamingly. "Each of you can merit the title Stakhanovite."

The prisoners eyed him coldly. This young man spent much time in the kitchen and store, in company with the camp officials. He had never shown excessive zeal when it came to doing his share of work, and they wondered at his enthusiasm for record-breaking tactics.

"Why should we want to be called Stakhanovites?" asked Hania, a sixteen-year-old girl with a mop of curly hair and a baby face.

"It is an honour," explained the baker's son. "A high achievement. . . ." He looked round rather helplessly at the blank expression on all the faces, and tried another slogan. "In the Soviet Union we workers have established an extraordinarily high level of accomplishment by means of the Stakhanovite movement."

"Surely," said Maria Wysocki in her pleasant lazy voice, "that's an old dodge; *we* call it pace-making . . . there are other terms, less pretty, too. Why are you so interested in our adopting Soviet methods?"

"You do not understand . . . you do not realize the extent of participation . . . the pride of ownership a Soviet worker feels. . . ."

Maria gave a low chuckle. "Surely, surely, I do, little man. Workers in this camp here own every bit as much. They too can say, *my* potato field; *my* forest; *my* swamp; isn't it so? That kind of ownership must make them yearn to be Stakhanovites."

"In Lemberg we had Stakhanovites working in the street cars, don't you remember?" said Olga. "Those drivers who were paid a bonus according to the greatest number of trips they made a day? People could hardly get on or off; the cars just flew along so quickly, not stopping at any of the halts. Half the time they ran empty, with would-be passengers making frantic signs for them to stop, and drivers stakhanoviting all along the route."

The prisoners laughed and the baker's son turned on them angrily. "I suggest we adopt the method here," he said. "We'll make a list of names and form the contingents."

He produced pen and paper, and much time was lost while names were being signed.

"But I don't want to put my name down," objected little Hania. "I don't want any title. I won't be a Stakhanovite."

"Oh, won't you?" threatened the baker's son, suddenly very sinister. There was an ominous silence; then he repeated, in even more menacing tones: "So you *refuse* to join the contingent?"

The guard on duty in the field intervened at this point. It was the Polish brigadier.

"I'd sign, if I were you," he said casually. "It's useless disagreeing about anything like this." His voice sank so low only the girl heard it. "It won't be a success anyway," he added. Then, turning to all the prisoners, he spoke authoritatively. "Now we will work on a competitive basis . . . each sets the pace for the other. You understand—Stakhanovite method; each sets the pace for the other." The baker's son smiled triumphantly and strode away. *He had put it over.* The brigadier continued looking fixedly at the prisoners. *"Each for the other,"* he repeated softly.

5. EXILES' FATE

It was nine o'clock on a Sunday morning. The queues before the store were smaller than usual, for the prisoners took advantage of this seventh (not holy) day to sleep an hour longer and entrusted their ration cards to someone who would try to do a little group shopping.

Henryk Fischer had for once taken his turn in line, instead of sending the Imp on this daily and much-hated job.

"Hi, you!" shouted the storekeeper, loading the bread into his arms, "tell the others in your cabin there's a meeting today at twelve, and everyone's to come."

"Where?" asked Henryk, paying no great attention to the woman's words.

"Clubhouse," was the curt answer.

"You go to numbers 12 and 18," continued the strident voice; and Henryk saw a young girl hurrying off in the direction of the cabins on the opposite side of the lane to his.

Word soon spread round the camp that Steputin would address a meeting at twelve o'clock; and to ensure a good attendance, the authorities closed the kitchen at that time so that no one would have the excuse of saying his dinner soup kept him from his duty.

A quarter of an hour before noon the prisoners began straggling into the clubhouse. One or two guards stood outside the picket fence around the yard where children had been playing with a flabby rubber ball; but even the children pushed into the hall when they saw the crowd gathering there. The benches were all full and men stood in groups near the windows and around the rail which separated the platform from the rest of the hall. Guards were on duty at the rail too, as though to prevent the crowds from getting too near the speaker.

A small wooden table and two chairs occupied the dais and the prisoners noted with hostile eyes the comings and goings of various Soviet officials who bustled about with a great show of importance. The more airs they gave themselves the more the Poles exhibited their complete lack of interest.

This psychic tug of war was never absent from the camp atmosphere, and on occasions like this it was naturally much in evidence.

By two o'clock Steputin had still not made his appearance, but the prisoners did not dare go away. They were always so hungry that the extra delay with their meal made little difference to their discomfort, but they bitterly resented the loss of time spent in the hall on their only day of leisure.

"This should be reckoned on our work schedule," grumbled Maria Wysocki, who never kept silent when she felt herself abused. "We should be recompensed for all these lost hours. And if we have to put up with Steputin's speech in addition, we deserve at least an extra pound of potatoes."

The Commandant came striding into the room at this moment and the ripple of laughter which had greeted Maria's words instantly died away. He mounted the platform and stood for a moment looking suspiciously at the audience. He wore a fine pair of high black leather boots, into which were tucked his dark blue riding breeches, his khaki tunic was open at the throat and his fair hair plastered down with an obvious attempt at elegance. A small blond man in pince-nez followed him onto the platform: this was Anton Minsk, a Polish engineer, one of the prisoners who had been chosen to act as interpreter, for Steputin would not speak Polish, though everyone in camp was convinced that he understood the language, and only professed ignorance of it to entrap prisoners into unwitting betrayals of themselves.

The buzz of talk subsided when he appeared, and even the children stood quite still, but there was no applause.

He broke into his speech without any preliminaries, and it was easy to see that he was not pleased with his audience.

"You Poles," he said, almost spitting the words at them. "You dirty Poles! You are not working nearly hard enough. You don't seem to realize what an opportunity we are giving you here . . . giving you work which is all for your own benefit. But the results are far from satisfactory. You will have to work much harder if you want to gain our approval. . . .

"You are all so dirty . . . you keep your cabins in such a disgraceful state. We are not going to tolerate such conditions in the camp any longer. You have to change them."

He sat down, glaring at his listeners with his narrow, fox-like eyes, peering at them sharply with an oblique glance, so that he could watch everyone in the hall without turning his head.

Minsk stepped forward to translate, but when he mentioned the dirt, there was a movement of indignation throughout the hall.

"If they'd sell us a little soap we might keep cleaner," murmured Olga.

"Of if there were a single scrubbing brush in the whole camp, it would help," added Maria, furiously. "Do you remember how they told us to clean the floors with our hands? Why do they ignore their part in our shortcomings?"

"It's they who are responsible for most of the dirt anyway; think of all that clay in the floor cracks," said Mrs. Fischer. "The more we wash the messier it gets."

"They just want to humiliate us," insisted Olga, "and prove that they are better than we are. It must give them tremendous satisfaction to be scolding us for something they know we all despise in them."

Steputin was on his feet again, resuming his speech, calling out the names of those who seemed especially to have incurred his wrath; mentioning a few who were not so bad as the others. Dr. Altberg was miserable when his name was among those whose cabins were considered to be decidedly beneath the high standard of Soviet cleanliness. He had hoped that ultimately he might be used as medical inspector, either at Zimny Gorodok, or in some other camp; and he was depressed and humiliated beyond measure when this chance faded with the public rebuke.

The Commandant was warming to his subject, waving his arms dramatically; he raised his clenched fists in the air, banged them on the table so that the glass of water rattled.

"*Grazny, grazny* . . . dirty!" He hissed the word like an angry goose. The children, who had been listening quietly enough at first, now began shuffling uneasily at his harangue, and one or two of them tried to slip away. But he turned on them roughly, shouting at them to keep quiet and stay where they were, and there was no mistaking the meaning of his tones, even if they did not understand his words.

"And don't imagine you are ever going back to Poland," he resumed, addressing his audience again. "That country is finished. It will never exist any more; and you had all better begin learning the Russian language, for you will never have a country of your own to go back to."

He went on a long time in this strain, talking about the victorious Red Army, the enduring might of the Soviet régime, and its superiority over all other forms of government. He worked himself into a white heat of passion when he dwelt on the extent of Communist power, quite unlike the stern, cold Steputin they had known hitherto, but even in the calmer translation of Minsk, his words sounded ominously final.

Holin, the work-giver, followed Steputin onto the platform. He had on a bright purple shirt for the occasion, and stood behind the table, with his heavy hands on it, leaning earnestly towards his audience as he exhorted them to work much harder.

The prisoners shifted wearily on their hard narrow benches.

"Now we are going to have that all over again," muttered Olga; and indeed it seemed that the "gaudy one" did nothing but repeat Steputin's words.

"You should realize that, after all, we ask you only to work for yourselves here," he insisted. "The potatoes you dig are for *you*; and the berries you pick are for *you*."

"That's another of their lies," observed Maria loudly, not caring who heard her. "The potatoes are strictly rationed; and as for the berries, they pay us fifty kopeks a day when we fill an eight-quart pail and then they try to sell them to us at one rouble fifty the pound. As if we could afford to pay for such luxuries!"

There was a general hubbub of disapproval all round her. The audience was getting exceedingly restive and showed the greatest reluctance to listen any longer. It was nearly four o'clock and everyone was very hungry and thinking of dinner.

The meeting came gradually to an end when the baker's son caused an unexpected diversion. He had been watching from the window the approach of a pale, dark youth who was dragging himself slowly towards the camp. This was an English boy, the son of a veteran of the last World War who had married and settled in Poland. The father and son had been arrested together, although the lad been been almost immediately transferred to Lejkin, where he had contracted tuberculosis and was being sent back.

His father, who wore a British service ribbon on his coat, was lame and had claimed exemption from camp work on account of his disability, but when he saw his boy, he went limping and lurching towards him, his arms outstretched, so delighted to see him still alive.

The baker's son, who was spying from the clubhouse, pointed and shouted at the sight.

"Look at him, look at the impostor!" he crowed. "He said he was lame and see how he runs!"

The Britisher was stumbling along, tears running down his cheeks. "Tom!" he cried, "Tommy-boy!" He could not cover the distance quickly enough to clasp his son in his arms.

"That's the way they deceive us!" yelled the baker's boy. "That's how they dodge their duties, the lazy swine! I'll show them!" And he rushed off, dragging one of the guards with him.

With this noisy exit the meeting petered out, and the prisoners moved over to the kitchen. They were crushed and sick at heart by the speech they heard. Long after they returned to their cabins Steputin's reproaches rankled; and his words on their country seemed to seal its doom.

Dr. Altberg sat down on his trestle bed, his head still ringing with misery.

"We did wrong in ever opposing Hitler," he said finally. "Poland should never have fought. Nothing could have been worse than our plight here. It would have been better to have accepted Germany's ultimatum in the first place."

"Why, how you talk!" expostulated Mr. Fischer. "We are not going to stay here forever. They say that just to get us down . . . to make us more pliable. Don't give in to them! If we hadn't stood up to Hitler when we did, Europe would never have had another opportunity of getting rid of the Nazis. If Poland had allowed itself to be swallowed by the Nazis like Austria and Czechoslovakia, nothing could have brought France and England into war with them. Ours was the last stand, and without us there might have been a Hitler-dominated Europe enduring for ages. And a fine chance we Poles should have had of ever recovering our independence under those conditions."

But Dr. Altberg would not be comforted.

"Then at least we should have accepted Russian nationality when we were offered Soviet passports in Lemberg. That would have saved us from a life like this."

"You are too short-sighted, my friend," objected Mr. Fischer, determined not to be affected by the other's pessimism. "What! Accept their nationality, after all we have been through! With no possibility of returning to a future Poland! Ah, no! We may have a bad time here, but it won't last, you mark my words. Possession of a Soviet passport would have been no guarantee that we wouldn't have been deported; but it would have effectively prevented our ever going back to rebuild our own country again. That is what we have to live for now. Poland will need us!"

His arguments finally dispelled much of the doubts and dejection of those in the cabin. Long weeks of isolation from every outside contact narrowed the prisoners' interests to a nagging perception of petty daily details; their lives were so monotonous that all other thought seemed stifled. This intellectual privation was harder to bear than anything else the Russians devised for the exiles; and at the end of a hard day's work, when fatigue and hunger sharpened their sense of desolation, the prospect of a thousand empty days before them was intolerable anguish.

No man lives, no man can live, without some object in view. The sensitive, introspective doctor had reached a point when almost all hope had fled, for his existence appeared meaningless to him. The afternoon's experience had been the final blow, and with characteristic melancholy he had identified the whole fate of his country with the personal rebuff he had received. Josef Fischer's vigorous reminder that Poland would have urgent need of men like himself, and that they must not fail her, was a valuable spur to his courage and stoicism.

The quality of his mind was apparent in its immediate reaction; he grew less morose, and when the two families united for an hour or so before preparing for bed, instead of the usual desultory conversation he began discussing the Bolsheviks, their aims and methods of propaganda.

"Take Steputin's talk today," he reasoned. "Does he really imagine he can permanently affect our outlook with such ideas?"

"We are too well fortified," responded Fischer, "but consider the case of the majority of Russians. They have no knowledge of the outside world . . . you remember their amazement at what they saw in Lemberg. They have been conditioned all their lives; there is no education that is not reduced to propaganda. All the widely advertised schemes for promoting popular culture and developing the masses, their workmen's universities and debating societies, amount to nothing more than the obfuscation of the truth. They distort reality by cramping it into a mould of officially organized opinion. That is why their reasoning processes seem so strangely illogical to us. They are like children or wonderfully trained monkeys who have learned to read and have acquired some curiously garbled pieces of knowledge, but seem incapable of associating ideas in a way familiar to the normally functioning brain."

Dr. Altberg remained silent for a moment, thinking this over.

"It is more serious than that," he said slowly. "The whole nation is suffering from intellectual and spiritual malnutrition. We doctors know what happens to physical organs when the body is deprived, over a long period, of adequate nourishment. But the harm is infinitely greater in the intellectual sphere when all constructive thought, investigation, and criticism are absent. In the first place, the country's economic life suffers on account of this: Russian industry, although undoubtedly highly proficient and developed in certain directions, is hampered by its incapacity to overcome elementary difficulties that demand independent judgment and its rapid application. This cannot be supplied when for years Russians have read, seen, and considered only what someone else has arbitrarily declared to be 'safe.' As for their general psychological condition, I tremble to think what abnormalities may develop under a system that condemns as 'contrary to the welfare of the State' all discussion and analysis of underlying problems. The reckoning, I fear, will be a heavy one."

"That reckoning will be made then in Germany as well," Fischer reminded him, "and in every country where the State assumes total and absolute control. Moreover, under this constant spiritual pressure, a pressure which is unrelieved by any of the compensatory possibilities afforded by literature and art, a generation is growing up totally lacking in self-imposed discipline, or in inner resources of any kind."

"True," observed Dr. Altberg. "The youth both in Germany and in this country possess no reserves of spirit or restraint. They boast of their lack of inhibitions, and rely on a fanatical devotion to a Leader, cutting themselves off entirely from the standards of traditional morality. But once let this fabulous Power-symbol, which they worship, fail them, or once let them begin to wonder whether their revolution is not too costly in terms of human suffering, then they are lost; they will break down. For there is nothing but emptiness within them. Yet their dissolution is inherent in the very creed they follow. When you set out to change by force the society in which you live, it is almost impossible to escape calculating the cost; or to avoid the tortuous inner struggle between loyalty to an abstract cause and the claims of common humanity.

"The Bolsheviks understand this only too well, which explains their hatred of democracy with its emphasis on the needs of the average man. They steel themselves to the belief that the end justifies the means, and dedicate themselves to the carrying out of a revolutionary program regardless of the barbarities it entails. Therefore, in their struggle for these abstractly conceived ends they cannot, they dare not, permit humanitarian heresies. . . ."

"Why, of course! That's it, isn't it?" exclaimed Olga, breaking in suddenly. "There's no love. That is what is so terrible in this country." She had been listening only half attentively; none of the women had followed in detail the discussion between the two men, but Olga had caught the last remark and something in Dr. Altberg's words and the tone of his voice quickened a luminous apprehension of all that she had felt and suffered in Siberia.

"Even under the Czar there was compassion . . . not much, of course, not widespread, but not forbidden. But the Soviets have *no* pity; they deliberately try to stifle what is noblest in people—that is the sin against the Holy Ghost. . . ."

In the evening light her face glowed, something fervent and intense flashed in her dark, shining eyes. Both men looked at her in silence. But before the conversation could be resumed the door opened noiselessly; Kurkof stood in the passage outside. His pock-pitted face was twisted into a scowl though he kept his hand on the latch as if he did not know whether to enter or withdraw.

"It is very late . . . and I have heard voices," he began. Everyone rose to their feet guiltily, unable to suppress a slight sensation of fear.

The Imp moved nimbly over to her father, giving him a little push in the direction of the door. "We were just going to bed," she said glibly to the guard. "It is late, as you say." She pursed her lips and gave an inimitable little parody of Steputin. "We shall do our best to sleep well in order to be strong enough to work hard tomorrow!" Kurkof's expression relaxed, and he turned to go. "Good night, *pan* Kurkof!" she called as he went out into the darkness.

Six peasants in a heavy rowboat pulled in at the jetty, shipped their oars, tied up the boat, and slowly climbed the steep banks to the camp of Zimny Gorodok.

It was the first time they had put in an appearance here and they approached the store with caution. They brought turnips, onions, and very skinny chickens for sale; and though they were supposed to deal only with the Soviet authorities, they all hoped to meet secretly some of the prisoners, and exchange their produce for something the Poles had brought with them from their own country.

In every Siberian peasant's consciousness was the deep conviction that outside Russia existed untold wealth. Stories of what travellers had left behind them; glimpses of prisoners in other camps all stimulated their curiosity and whetted their appetite for goods they could not obtain at home.

Safety pins now! That was a prize for an enterprising woman, if she could only dodge the guards and drive a little private bargain. Hairpins, too. The hairpins they bought in the village store were like clothes pegs, yet the peasants had seen Polish hairpins so dainty-light and choicely finished that you would have sworn they were fashioned for fairy folk. A pair of silk stockings . . . ah! That was something to dream of in vain! The women looked at their sturdy bare legs, under the shapeless colorless skirts they wore. They would give a pound of butter for a pair of silk stockings—and butter was worth forty roubles a pound.

They were ready to pay money, too, for any clothes the prisoners would sell them; what did they care how high the price? There was so miserably little on sale in all the surrounding districts that they lost all value sense of the paper roubles the government paid them to work the land. If only they could lay hands on some imported goods—leather that did not split the first time it was worn; dress material without flaws in every yard —they were willing to pay, whatever the cost.

Once a peasant had secured at a camp a pair of pyjamas that were the envy of all her neighbours; they were so fine she never put them on in bed. Not new, of course, but made of softest flannel; you could scarcely tell you wore them for they did not scratch at all. They were in two different shades of blue, and when you washed them the colors neither disappeared nor ran into each other; and of a cut so cunning it looked as though they followed the very lines of the body itself. She had gladly paid one hundred and sixty roubles for such a treasure. And the prisoner had seemed quite glad to let her have them, too.

The six peasants came shyly up to the camp, but it was dinnertime, and although the prisoners were not working in the fields, as they had feared, there were so many guards on duty, keeping the queues in order before the kitchen, watching the serving-woman who checked over the work lists (lest someone try to buy more than he had earned), the peasants felt sure there would be little opportunity of doing direct business and driving a good bargain.

They were quite right; the Soviet officials surrounded them almost immediately, and did their best to prevent any contact between them and the prisoners. They took the turnips, eggs, and other goods, paying them the nominal prices which they always gave to peasants. The Poles hovered about, realizing there would be no chance, this time, of doing a little barter. A very definite undercurrent of sympathy ran between them and the drab natives of this lonely land.

"Do you come from far?" Dr. Altberg managed to ask one of the men, as he was returning to the rowboat.

"From Schaborow, about five miles away," answered the man, looking carefully over his shoulder to see if he were being watched, and speaking as if he were not addressing the other at all. "That's the postal centre for this district. There were a lot of letters in yesterday. You may be getting some in a day or two."

Dr. Altberg rushed back to the cabin.

"Do you know what I've just heard?" he shouted. "One of the peasants told me there were letters for us at the post office. It's only five miles away, and he said he saw them there yesterday!"

They could hardly believe such good fortune. They had been two months in the camp, and it was more than ten weeks since they had left home; and all that time they had heard nothing of the outside world. They never knew if their own letters had reached their friends; they had had no reply or any sign of recognition. Now the news of possible mail circulated through the camp, and the whole place seethed with excitement. The prisoners did their best not to show their agitation, lest the Commandant note it and keep them longer in suspense. But when a postal official arrived at the camp three days later, and definite news went out that letters were actually there, the prisoners threw all pretence to the winds, and a wild crowd surged round Steputin's office. It was dinnertime, but nobody wanted to eat. They were in a ferment of expectation as they waited before his door, talking and laughing among themselves. They no longer felt isolated from the rest of humanity. They were like shipwrecked sailors to whom someone has thrown a rope. They clutched it fervently, not caring what was at the end of it, only thankful and delighted to be in contact with something again.

Steputin opened the door and looked at them icily.

"Mail will be distributed at five o'clock," he observed.

They went back to the kitchen.

They might have known that something like that would happen; yet, though Steputin's behaviour ran true to form, they could not conceal their bitter disappointment.

Excitement ran high again after they finished their work, but this time they were determined to master their emotion. It was a completely silent crowd that waited before the Commandant's house. About five-thirty he opened the door, and one by one they were allowed to enter.

Steputin sat in a straight-backed chair before a small wooden desk table. On it stood a rusty tin lamp with a glass chimney fixed in a wooden frame, which Mr. Fischer had made. The only other furniture in the room was also Fischer's handiwork—some rough shelves on which lay a number of folders and official-looking documents.

Olga's heart beat wildly as she stepped into the room.

"Is there anything for me?" she asked, hoping beyond hope that her American passport had arrived.

Steputin shuffled the entire bundle of letters through his hands, looking carefully at each address. He had obviously not sorted them alphabetically for it was not until he reached the last envelope that he looked up and said, "Nothing."

"Next," he called, before she was out of the room.

She walked slowly back to her cabin. She was terribly disappointed and anxious. She had written the American Embassy in Moscow the day after her arrival; and she could not bring herself to believe that they would have left her so long without a reply. She had given her letter to one of the men on the barges which brought the prisoners, begging him to take great care of it, impressing him with its importance; and he had seemed to show the utmost understanding, promising her faithfully to post it. Now she was tormented with the thought that perhaps her Embassy was still in ignorance of her whereabouts; and she wondered what assurance she would ever get that letters sent from the camp reached their destination.

With a heavy heart she entered the cabin: Henryk Fischer, his father, and Dr. Altberg were talking in low tones together.

"Henryk has received a letter from a student in Lemberg," said Dr. Altberg, as Olga came in. She could see that they were all very much perturbed, and she hardly liked to mention her own disappointment.

"I had to open it in front of Steputin," said Henryk. "He made us all open our letters and tell him from whom they came, but that was all. Typewritten letters apparently worried him, for he had Mr. Hind read the whole of a typed note he received, but it was only personal news and he made no comment. He may not have understood even. But I don't know what he would have said if he read mine. . . ."

Henryk held his letter in his hand, his face blank with horror, unable to concentrate on what he had just read. "I had no idea it would be like this . . ." he kept repeating, looking from his father to Dr. Altberg. "I never dreamed they were doing this to us."

He sat down heavily on the wooden bench, the letter falling from his fingers. His father picked it up and, with a gesture asking permission, began reading the closely written pages.

"Oh, is that a letter from home?" exclaimed the Imp, excitedly, coming into the cabin with her mother. The silence in the room was oppressive: she looked from one to another, her bright eyes darting over the scene, then deepening with a look so many of the camp children wore on their young faces.

"Is it bad news, Daddy?" she asked, clinging to his arm.

"It's pretty bad, darling," he answered, stroking her hair. He put the letter down and walked over to the window. "Our poor country," he murmured.

No one spoke at first; they all seemed choked, unable to discuss the contents of the letter. Olga offered to leave them, unwilling to trespass on their sorrow. But they would not hear of her going out again. "No, no," they cried, "it concerns us all. This is a national disaster."

They began talking in hushed and strangled tones, like those who know that death is in the house.

Henryk's letter was from a freshman at Lemberg University. It was written in a very guarded manner; in places it was even difficult to understand just what he intended to convey; evidently he had feared a strict censorship. It had been posted seven weeks after Henryk and his family were arrested, on the very day the writer had received a postcard from the camp. Mass deportations had taken place throughout all the country since then, wrote the boy; "twenty-two thousand from Lemberg alone," he said.

"We have had a letter from ——." The name was omitted, but a detail of description was added which made it easy for Henryk to identify a professor who had been among the first to be arrested and exiled the previous February. "He was five weeks on the journey in a sealed car, for it was shunted onto a siding and apparently forgotten. The station authorities threw a little food through the ventilation gratings, but three men died of cold and their bodies were not thrown out until the car was picked up and resumed its journey."

His train had encountered another full of Germans from the Volga settlements, who were being repatriated under the German-Soviet agreement. They were miserably dressed in tattered clothes, and the Bolsheviks, not wishing to let the Nazis see how the inhabitants of Russia lived, stripped the Poles of their good clothes and gave them to the returning Germans. The Poles had to take the Germans' rags in exchange.

"Several people in Lemberg have received news from exiles," continued the letter; "some have come from Kazakstan; there are thousands of Lemberg people there."

Dr. Altberg groaned as he heard this. "That's almost in Chinese Turkestan," he muttered; "it's a most appalling climate. Part of it is below sea level with terrific extremes of temperature; there is malaria everywhere, and a wind that cuts the skin to blood."

The letter concluded with greetings from several friends and acquaintances at the University: "You wouldn't recognize the place and classes . . . everything is so different now. 'Curly-top' has been called up for military service in the USSR Army." This was a sophomore whom they knew; "there was a general levy in a village on his uncle's former estate, but C. got an individual notice. They were all sent to Kiev and nothing has been heard from any of these recruits since."

Silence filled the room.

"I am going round to Rabbi Krantz," said Josef Fischer suddenly. "I saw him get a letter and I only trust his news is not as bad as ours. That poor stricken family!" He put on his hat and coat and felt his way along the dark, deserted lanes that ran between the cabins, knocking gently on the Rabbi's door. The old man himself opened it and Fischer's heart sank when he saw the haggard, tear-stained face.

"I have come to sit a little with you, my friend," said Fischer, taking the other's hand.

Rabbi Krantz returned the warm pressure, and led his guest into the front section of the cabin.

"I hope your wife is not suffering?" continued Fischer, using the formula all the camp inhabitants adopted when they spoke of old Mrs. Krantz.

"She is quiet now, I thank you," answered the Rabbi.

The little old lady still had spells of mania and violence, but most of the time she lay inertly on the wooden boards, her great brown eyes staring out of a face that had the cadaverous tautness of those about to die.

Since the arrest of her four boys she had hardly spoken a word, perhaps mercifully unable to understand the last great blow that had befallen her.

It was indeed a stricken family, as Fischer had said, for before they were all arrested in Lemberg, they had been living near Warsaw and had suffered brutal expulsion from their home at the hands of the Nazis. It was from German-occupied Poland that Krantz had received his letter. "I had to read it all through to the Commandant," whispered the Rabbi. "He seemed very suspicious when he saw the postmark, and I am surprised it was ever passed; but he only grunted something about its being a lesson to us all." He sat with the letter clasped in his hands, rocking to and fro, obviously relieved to have someone to talk to.

"Conditions at home are getting worse, the brutality in the concentration camps is increasing, but I am more worried about what they are doing to the young people in our towns than anything that they could possibly do to us," he confessed. "We already saw something of that before we left Warsaw . . . the deliberate debauching of youth . . . terrible, terrible. You see, Polish secondary and high schools have been closed so that girls and boys between the critical ages of twelve and fourteen have no mental or physical occupations at all. Many have been deported, for forced labour, of course, but those left behind are being subjected to an intolerable strain. Their parents in many cases have been sent away; they themselves live in constant dread of arrest; they are never sure of their next meal, and among these spiritual waifs the Nazis work with systematic thoroughness. The sale of alcohol is fostered everywhere and these children are encouraged to drink—payment for odd jobs is made in vodka; specially picked Polish-speaking "intermediaries" go about distributing obscene pictures and pornographic literature. You can see lads of fourteen and fifteen engaged in all kinds of shady business and illegal commerce; sometimes risking their lives trying to support some destitute relative; but often demoralized to the point of seeking only temporary forgetfulness. It is devilish . . . devilish." The old man rocked in his chair, words crowding his lips with the pent-up force of one who has too long schooled himself to silence.

He waved the letter in his hand, shaking his head. "One hundred shot . . . a hundred dead in the little market town of Wawer. . . . I know it well. Well, better so, I say, better that they die, than suffer further indignities." He leaned forward whispering, fearful lest he be overheard. "There was a clash there, between German soldiers and some Polish hoodlums . . . two Germans were killed, so a detachment of *Landeschützen* surrounded the place; a hundred random victims were dragged from their beds . . . into the market square . . . at night; by the light of head lamps from great police cars . . . they were machine gunned . . . while many of the townsfolk were forced to look on . . . and afterwards made to load the corpses onto farm carts and drive them to the cemetery . . . but even there the Nazis can take time out for their macabre humour; and Jews must be buried in Christian graves and vice versa."

He stopped suddenly, checking his voice that was rising to an angry scream.

"It will be the same everywhere . . . wherever the Germans hold us in power," he went on more quietly. "They will avenge themselves a hundred for one whenever we shoot. There will be man hunts; torture in concentration camps. But they cannot keep us in bondage forever; not unless they destroy us—a whole nation—altogether. . . ."

His eyes opened wide at the appalling picture he envisaged; and for a few moments he seemed communing with himself. Then he took Fischer's hand in his, pressing it gratefully. "You were good to come," he murmured, "I needed someone tonight. I have dwelt on our sorrows too long. . . . I forget . . . I forget. . . ." He began muttering something—prayers or curses—under his breath, and Fischer, gathering up his hat and coat, took his leave.

Mute despair hung over the camp for several days. At work the prisoners would not discuss their letters. Everyone had some idea of what was going on in

Poland, but they could not bring themselves to talk about the details: horror congealed the words in their mouths. They went about their work resentfully, but with frantic absorption, trying to blot out their memories by physical exhaustion.

Olga was tormented by fears that she had been forgotten or abandoned by the American authorities. She raked hay with wrathful determination. The brigadier moved over to her side: it was a Polish girl, Marysia, an agricultural expert, who had only recently been put in charge of a brigade. "Take it easy," she whispered to Olga. "You'll wear yourself out like that. Come and work by me where the ground is not so uneven."

The girl did her best to lighten Olga's task, choosing the best spots and keeping her out of the marshy stretches where the big flies and mosquitoes attacked the field workers till blood trickled down their bare legs. Ordinarily Olga would have been glad to take advantage of an opportunity to slacken. She was fond of Marysia, and snatching a moment's respite under a haystack the two had often discussed books and plays, lively interests they had both enjoyed before their exile. But now Olga obstinately continued tugging her rake through the heavy grass on the hill; and Marysia, who had been known to hearten her group with folk songs and encourage them to sing with her, did not insist.

And then the second batch of letters arrived.

The exiles heard about it with mixed feelings, for, eager as they were for news of home, they were reluctant to learn further horrible details of the treatment of their friends. As they stood before Steputin's house they were silent and cowed, like someone expecting a blow. Yet when the distribution had taken place, when they had read their letters, a general discussion blazed through the camp. They found themselves talking freely of their trials, perhaps because the element of surprise was no longer present and they had been psychologically prepared to meet this week's news, perhaps on account of the mounting wave of indignation that surged over them. Any kind of assembly was of course strictly forbidden, so they could not get together in large numbers; but there was a great deal of flitting from cabin to cabin after dark, for the exchange of information and views.

One letter was passed from hand to hand. It was written by a fifteen-year-old girl to an aunt in Lemberg who had forwarded it to her sister in Zimny Gorodok. The child had illustrated it with little sketches, a few rough lines with a blunt pencil on a rather dirty sheet of paper torn from a school notebook.

It came from Kazakstan.

"We live in a hole in the ground," wrote the girl. "It is quite a large hole, and wooden poles support the turf walls which are covered with dry clay and manure. We have a stove but it fills our hole with smoke. Yesterday two of us fainted. Our ceiling is so low that we can touch it with our hands and we have to crawl to go in and out. We are sometimes shaken with laughter at the way we are living; and then afterwards we weep. There are so many bugs and fleas we sleep with cotton in our ears.

"There is no permanent work here. W—— has been working in the stables. Mother and S—— and I have been embroidering linen. We worked all day for three weeks and earned enough to buy a pood [about 40 pounds] of potatoes. The Kirghiz are very wild looking, but some of them are kind to us. In all this village there are only two houses made of wood. Everyone lives in mud huts."

There was a picture of the interior of the "hole" with a clothesline in it from which hung a few garments. The struts supporting the sides and roof looked sturdy, though short; and three little figures were represented squatting near the opening, bending over their work.

Another letter from Kazakstan told of similar details.

"After twenty-two days we were brought to the Kirghiz steppe where there is nothing but grey emptiness. We live in a hut. The sun burns terribly; when it rains the hut leaks, all of our things are wet. We sleep on the ground; we have no beds, no tables, no chairs. We work all day till we fall. Then we cannot sleep for the bugs. We have been forced to work on the dungheaps, as that is the main work here, mixing dung by hand with fertilizer eight hours a day, even during the worst heat. The only reward once every ten days is a kilo of black, sour flour."

Some of the letters quoted news received from Siemipalatynskaja, in the same district; the living conditions were equally hard, thirty people living together underground, beneath a peasant's hut. Manure was the mainstay of life: made into cakes, it was the only form of heating; mixed with sand and clay it formed the chief building material.

"Today we carried twelve hundred pails of water from

the river and emptied it into barrels. For work like this we are paid twenty-eight roubles a month; and white flour costs one hundred roubles a pood."

A former Polish landowner's wife recounted: "We hauled wheat, four tons daily, in and out, spreading it on linen sheets to dry in the sun, then back in sacks and into the hut at night. We work in the fields with bullocks for tractors; they are so stubborn, so melancholy, you cannot imagine. I have been made chief of our brigade. There are nine people sleeping in our room, which is twenty-five metres square.

"We live in a large village of mud huts, half the population is Mongolian. The village Soviet has issued us Russian passports good for five years. It is very dry, and we all suffer from headaches. We feel there is nothing we do not experience, that we are passing through a wonderful school of life. There is a strange beauty here, wonderful colour, and the natives find plenty of game. Send us books, we beg you. Everything here is so dear, we do not eat much, but yesterday I exchanged a chemise for thirty quarts of milk."

One little girl said she had sold all her handkerchiefs: "We look like dried sticks." The children in her colony were employed collecting resin from pine trees; for one hundred pounds of resin they received two pounds of bread. In another camp children worked like horses, but were growing into "regular savages and brigands," they were so hungry.

Everyone expressed fear of the coming winter: "We cannot last beyond spring. . . . Perhaps God will work a miracle; everything is nothing if only we can hope.

We only live by bartering our clothes. What will happen to us when we have no more to sell?"

"Please pray for me," wrote an old lady of seventy-three. "If I die here, say a mass for me. I do not want to be buried in the mud."

"We make shoe polish here from soot. There are lots of nettles and we eat them," wrote a professor's wife.

A man of sixty-three had written from Archangel Province, where the deportees were engaged in forestry. Although he was a skilled forester and in addition an engineer speaking fluent Russian, no attempt had been made to employ him in any of the work connected with forestry. "I have been kept mending roads since my arrival," he complained, "this in spite of my bad leg."

"Don't stay in Lemberg," advised another man, from the Taiga forest. "Go to the green frontier [into German-occupied Poland]. Here we are building barracks for forty thousand more people who are expected from Lithuania, Estonia, Bessarabia, and Buchovina."

"Evidently he does not know what is going on in German-occupied Poland," commented Rabbi Krantz dryly, when this last letter was under discussion. He had recovered his equanimity. A stern light flamed in his eyes, lines grooved his cheeks from nostril to chin, but he spoke quietly and with mastery over himself. He sat with the Altbergs and the Fischers long after the light had faded.

"This looks like an attempt at systematic extermination of a whole people," he said conclusively. "From the little we know, we can guess the rest. It is only beginning now. God help us when our oppressors get through."

"When Poland was partitioned before, at least they didn't touch the people," said Olga hotly.

"That was the great mistake, according to the Germans," said Rabbi Krantz. "Then, both the Poles and their hopes were left intact, which led to the resurrection of their State. In 1918, at the moment of Brest-Litovsk, when a German victory seemed clear, Hindenburg declared, 'It is necessary, once and for all, to remove all basis for Polish ambitions, and make them dependent on the support of the German Empire.' Stalin seems to have taken a leaf out of the old Marshal's book."

"The Russians certainly aim at making conquered peoples dependent on the State," commented Dr. Altberg, a rising acerbity strident in his voice. "Their economic disorganization has led to a wilful pauperization of the urban population; and by collectivizing the peasants and destroying their ties with the land, they have transformed these people into nomads without property, family, or place in the world. And as if this were not enough, they instituted mass deportations, which, in spite of everything they say, are of a purely political character.

"Would they be sending civil servants, intellectuals, men from the liberal professions, into the wilds of Siberia if they were merely interested in land settlement?" His voice rose to a shriek as though challenging Fate to give him an answer. "If this were the case, wouldn't they have chosen agricultural labourers and foresters? Or used the deported engineers to some purpose? No, they are doing this solely to de-Polonize the country, to destroy once and for all the chance of there ever being a class capable of bringing about its revival."

He broke off, strangled with emotion. And the four men looked at each other with a realization of sickening certainty. A devil of black fury whipped them to a blazing pinnacle of anger where reason and revolt fused in a fearful incandescence. Lawyer, doctor, rabbi, and student, honourable components of their country's heritage, turned their gaze on the narrow confines of their log-cabin prison, trapped and impotent.

Dr. Altberg struck his forehead with the flat of his palm and lifted his hand accusingly to heaven, tongueless with rage; Henryk, his shoulders humped and hopeless, hands thrust deep in his pockets, bit his lips till a bloody line showed on the taut skin.

His father slipped his arm round the bowed figure, and caught Dr. Altberg's hand with a restraining solacing gesture.

"More than ever, my friend, more than ever, we must live through this trial; we must cling to our health and our sanity to be ready to give what we can. . . ."

The Rabbi's deep-set eyes travelled from the two men and rested upon the lad.

"Vengeance is mine, saith the Lord."

He muttered the words with sombre emphasis, and walked out of the cabin.

6. MEMORIES

Three times the red-bearded postman brought mail to Zimny Gorodok. He dumped his sack of letters on the long table in the shack behind the kitchen which served as dining room and store; and while he waited for Steputin to come and check the load he gulped down hot tea, potatoes, and jam, his long legs spread out in front of him, his feet swathed in felt and shod in birch bark laced with leather thongs.

For three weeks the prisoners had been receiving letters, but Olga was still without news from Moscow. Her anxiety increased as days went by, for her only hope of release lay in the repossession of her American passport. Though Steputin professed to believe her story of American citizenship, it was quite obvious that he was prepared to do nothing about it until he had seen her "document." Until this arrived, she was just another political exile, and never had the little red folder seemed so desirable, so all-powerful, as when viewed from the inside of a Siberian prison camp.

Her first steps to obtain it had been in January, 1940,

when a Mr. Ward, member of the American Embassy in Moscow, had visited Lemberg to assist those Americans who found themselves stranded in Russian-occupied Poland.

It had been a long time since she had required American papers, for in the good old days before the World War passports were treated lightly and afterwards she generally travelled on her husband's. Now it was a very different story. Mr. Ward gave her numerous application forms to fill out; she made the necessary payments, and waited hopefully for the precious result.

He had returned to Lemberg the following March and summoned her immediately. Radiant with expectation she presented herself at the American Consulate only to learn that she must fill out yet more questionnaires. New conditions required new formalities, explained Mr. Ward; and the passport seemed as far off as ever.

Then came the letter from Moscow definitely stating that it would be issued and would be ready in three months. It was this letter that she had vainly endeavoured to show to the Soviet authorities at the moment of her arrest, but they paid no attention to it at all.

Three times since her imprisonment she had written and telegraphed Mr. Ward, and when two months passed and the mail still brought no reply she was convinced some dreadful complication had arisen or that for some reason or other her passport had been cancelled.

Every imaginable fear seeped into her consciousness, draining her courage; for days she went around petrified by the belief that she would never regain her freedom. This obsession paralyzed her waking thoughts so that all movement seemed arrested and she could no longer even formulate the desire to be free. She felt suspended in space, like a creature in a slowed-up film condemned to infinitely-drawn-out drudgery.

But a crisis of nerves like this rarely lasted long. Her own vigorous common sense and the compassionate friendliness of those about her banished such spectres. Dr. Altberg emerged from his own despair when Olga stood in need of encouragement; Josef Fischer's sanguine humour was never so reassuring as when his lonely neighbour needed comforting.

"Don't let this life get you down," Maria Wysocki would whisper as they worked together; "keep on top of it; you'll win out; you'll get away."

Sometimes Maria's own courage would ebb and then it was Olga's turn to be strong for them both; or even the jovial Fischer occasionally would falter, for though he never mentioned it to his wife, the forced labour was beginning to affect his heart, and there were terrifying moments when he confessed his suspicions to Olga and it needed all her energy and self-reliance to restore his equanimity.

This mutual sustenance and incitement to fortitude was the stuff of their lives. It bound them together as nothing else could have done; against this gallant background they wove their daily round of tedium, pain, and drained heartsick humiliation and terror. But for this concerted courage many a weak soul, tired of the living death, would quietly have hanged himself in his cabin.

Recent letters to the camp, however, had revived in Olga a hope she had hardly dared entertain before. Many of the prisoners had received good news of relatives believed lost in the war. The German blitzkreig had been so ruthlessly unexpected that whole regiments had seemed annihilated by it; yet many officers and men, defeated and dispersed, had found their way back to safety.

They had fought with a fantastic bravery which was not universally appreciated until the lightning collapse of the French made the world realize what prodigies of staying power the defenders of Poland had shown. And now their endurance and tenacity were once more demonstrated by the fact that whole units, with their sidearms, slipped from the German clutches, and got away and out of the country to continue the fight elsewhere.

Was it possible, Olga wondered incredulously, that Jan too had escaped? Was her Johnny still alive, unharmed somewhere, and free?

The postman who had dashed her own hopes of release so utterly furnished this wondrous new possibility. It became the chief focus in her life, a new incentive for living. She would count her days fulfilled, she felt, if she could only survive to know the truth about her son. Her imprisonment might even be serving some inscrutable purpose, she decided, on the assumption that the invasion of a country inevitably brought about a great deal of misery; and now a new prayer was seldom absent from her heart: "Oh, keep Jan safe, dear God; let me take all the suffering if it must be so, but bring him back safely, O Lord."

Olga was fundamentally religious, but her exile was a daily challenge to her belief in the ultimate goodness of things. Her acceptance of the Divine Will did not preclude speculation as to the reasons for her suffering. "Why has this happened to me?" she continually asked herself.

During the short light summer nights, when sleep had been so fragmentary, the question haunted her ceaselessly.

Rabbi Krantz had said: "We have sinned, we must atone." But Olga, searching her heart, was not conscious of any sin. Her happy busy life seemed to offer so little in support of the gloomy Jewish view. Had she failed as wife or mother? Was happiness itself a sin?

In camp there were no other interests to take her mind from this problem: back it came as daylight faded and she faced the lengthening nights alone.

Perhaps she had taken happiness too much for granted? And had she not taken love for granted too? How often had she remained silent, unresponsive to Waclaw?

Was love something so important it *must* be made manifest? Was it a sin to curb one's ardour, hide its full expression?

Under normal circumstances she would never have indulged in such searching introspection. She would have considered it morbid. But now, when she was so achingly aware of the hard plank bed beneath her and of the morrow's hateful task, she found she had no armour against self-examination.

Sometimes, in the dark log cabin, Dr. Altberg would hear from Olga's bed in the opposite corner a low, stifled sob. It was so quiet and despairing his heart was nearly broken at her distress. He longed to be of service to her, but he knew he was helpless to comfort her, even had the presence of his wife and daughter not made the attempt impossible.

How many sleepless nights had he not listened to her grief; and how often had she cried, not for her present plight, but for the lost happiness she had never fully acknowledged?

Music had been her passion, and love of Waclaw was merged in her love of music.

Even at school in Chicago she had spent far more time playing the violin than she had ever given to her studies.

Her father encouraged her, for at heart he was a musician too, and all the hours he could spare from his busy doctor's life he devoted to his cello. He was a tremendous worker, a loving tyrant, and a great idealist, was the fiery Kazimir Butkiewicz.

"Never forget," he told Olga and her sister in those early days in the great braggart city, "money is nothing, but wealth of knowledge is always yours." And for his two gifted daughters he engaged private tutors to supplement their school work with music, foreign languages, art, dancing, for he was determined they should be rich indeed.

It was a gay, satisfying life they led on the South Side, by the University, and later on the near North Side. Olga's mother was a pianist and came from a long line of musicians: there was always music in the house all day long, string quartets and dazzling solos, grand opera—for Olga's sister Irene had a magnificent voice.

Irene was the belle of the family: artists begged to paint her portrait; scores of photographers tried to do justice to her mobile expressive features. Olga grew up listening to the compliments they paid her, and shared their admiration for this dearest of companions. Her pride in her sister's good looks made her unaware of the appeal of her own eyes, and blind to the shining pallor of her own more subtle beauty, fed inexhaustibly from within.

When she was seventeen Olga won the highest award for violin, a gold medal from the Chicago Musical College. She had studied with Hermann and Sauret but wanted to finish in Europe. It was after she had listened attentively to the pupils of various famous masters that she decided to go to Poland and work with Waclaw Kochanski.

"That's the maestro for me," she declared without any hesitation, and set off for Warsaw to present herself at its Conservatoire there.

She had been reckoned Chicago's most brilliant student, but at her first encounter with a European celebrity she could hardly suppress a feeling of nervousness.

Kochanski listened quietly while she played to him for nearly an hour—the Wieniawski études; some Bach; Schubert's *L'Abeille*; the *Canzonetta* of Sauret; half a dozen show pieces to prove her technical brilliance. Never once during her performance did he take his eyes from her. His thick hair was flung back in a dome of living jet; a heavy moustache did not conceal the sensitive curve of his mouth.

Under his steady gaze Olga's heart began to beat

faster and she played as she knew she had never played before. Her tone flowed warm and clean, pulsating with her rising excitement, but never losing its golden rounded quality. Finally she laid down her instrument, waiting a little breathlessly for his comment.

"Good," he said slowly, looking at her with dreamy intensity. "Very good indeed . . . the right arm is perhaps . . . a little stiff. . . ."

She went back to her room, her heart pounding in her ears. Never had she met anyone whose personality had so immediately impressed her. She could not rid herself of the memory of his eyes, and the passionate, brooding concentration of his face. She kept hearing the sound of his voice, though he had spoken so little. "Good," he had said, "very good"—the words were like a caress—"but the right arm is stiff." And he had shown her how he wanted her to hold her arm. She remembered his hands, with the immensely long thumb and fingers, and their suggestion of supple vibrant strength.

How she worked, all that week, how the notes flew under her excited fingers; what hours she practised with the right arm relaxed, trying to attain that optimum of controlled and free action that he demanded from her bow.

She lived only for the next lesson; she could think of nothing else but seeing him again. The week seemed endless, yet all time was spinning madly.

And then came a note; just a formal announcement, though she tried in vain to read into it something personal and intimate. He was leaving for Warsaw for a concert, and her second audition would be postponed.

Was it possible that life could be suddenly so blank

because a violin lesson must be missed? Could the presence of one person possibly make such a difference to her existence?

She shook herself out of a romantic reverie. All little pupils, she told herself sharply, were probably equally impressed by the great artist and master teacher. There was no reason, she scolded, for this feeling of black emptiness just because he left the city for a few days.

She schooled herself diligently for their next encounter and was prepared to carry it off with an imperturbable manner. She felt quite cool and collected all the time the master was speaking to her, discussing at length her programme of work; but when she picked up her violin to begin playing to him she felt his eyes envelop her again; their warmth flowed over her in a strong current, and her self-possession vanished. During their conversation she had found it possible to look right into those dark great pools; she had not faltered but met his gaze frankly, her grey eyes holding his, neither challenging nor shy. But when he ceased speaking and there was nothing but music between them, then she was engulfed in their fiery flood; her body swayed and trembled with emotion; she dropped her eyes and whirled her bow across the strings, taking refuge in music to quell the tumult within her.

Two months passed, with two or three more lessons, then her mother and sister arrived from Chicago and she joined them for a long vacation of travel. They visited all the places she had always longed to see: Rome, Venice, the Salzkammergut; they toured the fabulous picture galleries of Paris, Madrid and Amsterdam; they climbed Swiss mountains and sailed in the fiords of Norway. It was all so wonderful and she was ashamed that in this new and exciting world she found herself longing impatiently for her return to Lemberg.

They were in Vienna, about to depart for London, where Dr. Butkiewicz was to have joined them, when a telegram informed them abruptly of his death. He had succumbed to blood-poisoning after performing a brilliant operation in which he had cut his hand slightly.

The girls and their mother were overwhelmed with grief. It was doubly tragic that he should have died this way—the first time they had ever left him. And Olga felt additional remorse, as though she had somehow failed him, for he would have wanted her to profit so much by all her travel.

Their plans for England were cancelled, and Mrs. Butkiewicz was making her melancholy preparations for an immediate return to Chicago when Olga received a letter with a Lemberg postmark.

Waclaw Kochanski had learned of the death of his pupil's father and tendered his heartfelt condolences.

He wrote with such touching warmth and sincerity that Olga wept anew and showed the letter to her mother.

"That must be a very lovely and exceptional man," said Mrs. Butkiewicz, wiping her eyes, "to have found time in his busy life to write like that to a pupil he hardly knows."

She was loathe to leave her little daughter in Europe now, and clung to her tearfully as they bade each other farewell.

Olga went back to Lemberg, a silent, woebegone

little figure, her black dress throwing into even greater relief the white, glowing brightness of her skin.

She made her home with a college professor's widow who boarded several musical students: her friend was there, Maria Zaleska, whose brother was later to become Poland's Foreign Minister, and the girls followed a rigorous schedule of practice and work; all day the house rang with singing and the sound of students' instruments; evenings they devoted to concerts and opera. They were delighted to have an American among them and Olga was soon absorbed into the strenuous stimulating life, gradually forgetting her loss.

She went back to Kochanski for lessons. At their first meeting he had not spoken of her father, but he held her hand so long between his own, his head bowed and almost touching hers, she was sure he understood her sorrow. Before he let her go he seemed about to stroke her hair, and Olga longed to feel his caress, but he drew himself stiffly from her, and picking up the violin, handed it to her with a formal little bow for the lesson to begin.

Once when she had finished playing he detained her for a moment.

"Do you understand Polish well?" he asked.

"Yes," she answered, wondering at his question, for he always spoke so little to her.

"But when you read it, do you understand every word?" he insisted.

"But yes," she breathed, startled by his tone.

He took a letter out of his pocket and put it into her hands, holding them both between his own and drawing her so close that she did not dare look up into his face.

"I want you to read this," he whispered, "but only when you are quite alone. I want you to read it very carefully and tell me what you think of it at your next lesson."

She lifted her eyes but dropped them immediately, afraid of what she saw, yet even more afraid that she might be mistaken after all.

She held the letter tightly in her hand in the street-car, not daring to open it there, yet hardly able to restrain her impatience and longing to read it. But when she reached home it was already late, and the girls were waiting for her to go to the theatre.

"Make haste, Olga," they shouted. "We thought you were never coming. We mustn't miss the first act." They hovered around her as she snatched a sandwich and hurried off to see *Peer Gynt*. The letter lay in her pocket, but she had no opportunity to read it.

All through the play she wondered about its contents, turning it over with burning fingers, her feeling of frustration growing that there was no moment when she could be alone.

When the curtain finally fell she threw on her wraps and hurried back to the house. But there was the usual jolly foregathering of all the students; they made tea and sat around discussing the drama, chattering and criticizing; it would be hours before they went to bed. Olga went into the bathroom and locked the door. She was trembling with excitement as she broke the seal on the envelope.

It was a passionate love letter. His words poured out

of his heart. He had loved her, he told her, from the first minute she had played to him, from the very moment that he set eyes on her. Never had he felt such love for anyone before. She must tell him if she cared, if she thought she could ever care at all for him. He could not go on without knowing what she felt. Sometimes, when she played, he was filled with wildest hopes, she seemed so close, so very much his own. Then the dazzling warmth vanished and he was bewildered and alone in the dark cold, and could only beg her to tell him the truth.

Whatever her answer, he would remain her devoted teacher; nothing should interrupt her studies for the brilliant future he was sure was hers. He realized she was very young. He would be patient and understand; she could rely on him. But silence was no longer possible; he had to declare his love.

She read it twice, three times, covered it with kisses; then crushed it guiltily into her pocket and joined the others.

"Where have you been?" they clamoured. "What kept you so long?"

"You look so absolutely radiant," observed Maria Zaleska; "whatever has happened?"

Sleep was impossible that night. She was too excited, too happy. She could hardly believe that the great Waclaw Kochanski really loved her. It was not a schoolgirl's fancy, then, the smouldering passion in his eyes.

She wanted to go to him immediately, to give him her answer. She had no need for lengthy consideration. Why had he said "at the next lesson"? Must she wait so long?

Yet she did not dare interrupt his courses: she was still unfamiliar with his timetable at the Conservatoire; pupils came to him from all over Europe, and she was too timid to do anything but just what he had told her.

And at the next lesson she was even a little late. She had planned to be there so promptly, but time slipped by while she was dressing and she missed the streetcar.

He was pacing up and down the room when she arrived and turned on her almost fiercely when she opened the door.

She did not say a word. She could not speak. She never knew how she found herself in his arms, with his mouth crushed against hers.

"Olga . . . Olenka . . . *kochanie moje!*"

He rained kisses on her lips, her eyes, her throat. He held her face in his strong hands to read the answer for himself. He clasped her so tightly she felt she would faint with pleasure; then he released her, an infinite tenderness succeeding his passion. He looked into her face adoringly as he took her hands in his, kissing each finger separately.

"Olga . . . little golden one. . . ."

She was melted by this change of mood, by his whispered endearments and the mobile play of his face as he told her how he loved her.

There was no lesson that day, and little enough work during the next two months. Waclaw was like a schoolboy playing truant: every moment he could steal from his music he spent with her; they had so much to talk about, so many tastes in common to discover; they wandered about the city hand in hand telling no one of their happiness.

"But why don't we get married at once, Olga?" he begged. "I had to wait so long till you came into my life. When I think of all my years without you!"

He did not want a wedding in Lemberg; he was too well known to have escaped without a crowd, but out in the country there was a tiny church near the home of someone who already shared their secret. Madame Ostrowska insisted on planning the wedding breakfast: she was director of the School of Music and Waclaw's oldest friend. Was it she who whispered a word to his students? Or was the maestro's radiant face its own betrayal?

When Olga arrived at the church that summer morning it was covered inside and out with roses, and a full string orchestra played her up the aisle. She was moved to tears by the beauty of the scene, the flowers, the students' music. Waclaw was all tender bewilderment as she sobbed and clutched his hand convulsively.

"Maybe you don't want to get married?" he suggested wistfully.

She laughed then and kissed his troubled eyes. And afterwards everything went very merrily indeed.

There had always been roses in their first home in the Listopada Ulica and a summerhouse on the lawn banked with violets and roses, where Olga was soon taking her part in the string quartets that played there two or three times a week. Waclaw even held out hopes of a concert début.

Not that all her time was given to music. Waclaw

was a versatile companion: they made long excursions to the Tatra Mountains, and in the Carpathians, for he loved to climb, and they hiked and walked together; in winter they skated miles over the frozen river and lakes round Lemberg; there were gay Bohemian parties. Olga prided herself too on her domestic virtues: she was determined to be no child-wife. Her cooking was the toast of his musical cronies, but she modestly disclaimed their extravagant praise.

"Why shouldn't I have a light hand with pastries and *piroshkis* since Waclaw perfected my flying staccato?"

They roared with delight; for Waclaw's staccato bowing was nationally famous; though there were some who whispered that hers would one day rival his.

And then the great moment came for her first public appearance as a soloist. The Narodowa Sala was crowded to the last seat by Lemberg's musical élite, for more than ordinary interest was aroused by the romantic young American girl who had captured the heart of their beloved Kochanski.

She looked a very frail figure when she stepped onto the podium of the great concert hall. She was to play the Max Bruch *Concerto in G minor* with the Philharmonic Orchestra, and as she stood grasping her violin, very straight and still in a Grecian gown of palest green crêpe, the audience saw her look into the stage wings and smile. They did not guess that just before her appearance she had been so nervous that she had almost fainted and was convinced that she could never go through with the programme. She faltered and trembled with fear while the orchestra waited for her.

Waclaw held her hands and looked at her sternly.

"Do you believe what I tell you?" he asked.

"Yes . . . yes, always," she whispered.

"Then I tell you you will *not* be nervous when you face your audience."

He raised her chin, smiling into her eyes, then with a swift kiss and a little tap behind he urged her towards the stage. Unseen by the audience he watched her intently all the time she played.

She was a brilliant success.

The critics immediately recognized her highly musical temperament, while her technique was all, and more, than they expected from a Kochanski pupil. They overwhelmed her with praise and outdid each other with compliments. "It is difficult to know which to admire most, the elasticity of the bow or of the body," wrote one who was usually extremely severe with budding musicians.

The public applauded clamorously and Waclaw was justly proud of her, but it was two years more before he allowed her to appear with him in public. Then, at the Conservatoire at Warsaw, they played the great Bach concerto for two violins together, and he entrusted the first part to her. That was one of her greatest triumphs. Never would she forget the particular thrill of that evening as she stood by his side facing the big hall. A golden haze of light enclosed them, palpitating magic brilliance; and beyond it was the audience, excited, nervously responsive, as though they too were aware of the deep musical bond between the two violinists, the tension that beat in unison like the throb of a great pulse.

Against the sheer virtuosity of Waclaw's sustaining

arpeggios her cadenzas climbed in increasing emotional power, fuller, more glowing, till the two instruments soared in ever greater imaginative flights and contrasted terraces of tone to the exultant finale.

Never, said the critics, had the concerto been played with such inner harmony or musicianly understanding.

When they played together all barriers seemed to be down. At such moments Waclaw could never have doubted her absolute love for him. After such moments, life could offer no more.

But it was not enough for her.

She wanted a child.

Waclaw was far less enthusiastic at the prospect: he had found life so very sweet and he feared that with her responsibilities of motherhood he would lose his darling playmate. Yet when Jan was born it was Waclaw who rejoiced most; and the rare qualities which his pupils had long since discerned in him and which had won him their loving sobriquet of "father," were now devoted to his own little son.

Life seemed too complete. Olga was almost fearful of her happiness; yet, even then, near-tragedy was only around the corner.

They were spending the summer at Waclaw's father's estate, Wisnowcik, in Russian Poland, when one evening they were suddenly surprised by a disturbing clank of spurs. The house was surrounded by soldiers, and three officers, with drawn revolvers, ordered Waclaw's immediate arrest.

Olga could not believe her senses at this unjustified intrusion. Without warrant or explanation they drove off with him to the nearest town and he was flung into prison. She was frantic with anxiety, and only after three days did she learn that he had been seized because some student from Lemberg University was accused of having publicly burnt the Czar's portrait.

"But it is fifteen years since Waclaw was a student there!" she exposulated, unable to understand how such an enormity could occur. ". . . And on the very day that the 'crime' happened he was giving a concert at Kaminiec, as a thousand people could testify!"

She besieged the governor with demands and petitions, reckless of consequences and her own safety; nevertheless, he was left in his cell twenty-two days. He could order his meals from town and Olga was allowed to visit him; but otherwise he was treated as a political prisoner.

It was the ceaseless efforts of his father, who appealed personally to the Minister of the Interior, that won his release. As unceremoniously as he had been arrested, was he now turned loose. Olga, with her American conceptions of justice and personal security, was horrified by this example of "barbarous lawlessness," as she called it, but Waclaw took the incident more philosophically.

"I suppose it had to happen to me," he said dreamily, "in order that *that* note might be in my music."

He could accept danger for himself with equanimity, but when Olga was threatened, that was a different matter; then it was he who suffered and quailed and she who was bravely calm.

They were living in Kiev when the Bolshevik revolution broke, and Soviet troops approached the city. One of the local landowners, Jaworski, father of one of

Waclaw's pupils, had invited them to spend the summer on his estate, and Olga was there when an armed band was reported marching on the property. Jaworski, like so many of his kind, could not imagine that he would be molested: he had always treated his peasants well; they were loyal and happy and he saw no menace for himself in the social changes. He waited in his villa to receive the deputation, but Olga and his married daughter decided at the last moment to leave, and with their babies made a precipitous and adventurous flight, taking refuge in a priest's house in a neighbouring village.

Jaworski and his household were brutally murdered; so was his nearest neighbour, Prince Sapieha. Their mutilated bodies were found afterwards, the eyes wide open and transfixed with horror, for they had been buried while still alive.

Shaken by her narrow escape, Olga was rescued by Waclaw, who came to take her back to Kiev.

"Olga . . . my little Olus! How could I have lived if you had been killed?" he shuddered. It was as if she had returned to him from the grave. They clung desperately to each other as dangers and disasters piled up around them. He could hardly bear to have her out of his sight; if he left town, he called her half a dozen times a day. The Soviet troops entered Kiev and there was fierce hand-to-hand fighting in the streets. Peril was part and parcel of their existence then; every day death threatened, and each thought only of the other.

One winter night a group of rough soldiers forced their way into her house just as she was giving Johnny his bath.

"There was firing from your windows," they declared. "We are being treacherously attacked from your house."

"Impossible," she countered quickly. "No one could have shot at you from here. All our windows are sealed." (In good Russian fashion, with the first frost, all cracks were papered over.) "Search the house and see for yourselves," she added, hoping to get these ferocious-looking individuals out of the room before they discovered Waclaw.

But dragging him with them, they clumped off to investigate. "If we find any arms, we shall rip your bellies open," they shouted.

She finished putting Johnny up to bed, then sat down suddenly, paralyzed with sickening dread. The shotguns and hunting rifles which some friends had stored with other valuables in her attic! She had forgotten all about them!

A terrified servant tiptoed in to announce that the Bolsheviks had just discovered them.

"They will kill Waclaw!" was her first thought, and her heart almost stopped beating. "I must go and explain . . ." She rushed upstairs, gasping with terror. "They are not ours . . ." she shouted; "those are not our arms. . . ." She did not see Waclaw at first when she dashed into the attic and feared he was already slain; but she stopped short when she caught sight of what was going on. The Bolsheviks had smashed open all the trunks and packing cases; the floor was littered with clothes, furs, costly objects—all in wildest disorder. The soldiers were laughing and yelping with delight and, in true Banderlog fashion, seemed to have forgotten all their former ferocity and the firearms.

"We come with a cart and take all this away," they announced to her gleefully, and in very short order they marched off with the booty.

It was too much for her; she collapsed into Waclaw's arms when they disappeared, weeping and clinging to him. Finally she allowed him to persuade her to leave the country. At the first opportunity she escaped to America and went to Chicago again to live.

Twice Waclaw came over to her for long periods and gave concerts throughout the country: she begged him to stay in the United States, to make it his home, to learn something of its comfort and security, but successful as he was, he could not be happy there. Now there was a free Poland to go back to, his longing for his own country was too great.

He walked the bright boulevards of Chicago, oblivious of the people, tears thick in his eyes. "I cannot stay. I must give the best in me to Poland," he said simply; and Olga knew she could never persuade him to do otherwise.

He returned to Warsaw, and became the director of its Conservatoire, and in 1924 Olga and Jan rejoined him. And in the old grey building of the Conservatoire, hallowed by the memories of Paderewski and other great artists who studied there, they lived in an apartment overlooking the century-old trees in its rambling gardens, with windows from which they could see the fast-flowing Vistula.

Fifteen happy years went by. Yet, looking back on them now, Olga wondered if their uninterrupted tranquillity had not robbed her of something very precious. As the flame of danger slowly receded had not her own nature grown chill, insufficient to her passionate husband? Her playing still revealed the fire within her; she, perhaps, more than he, could pack into music feelings her lips could never utter; but now that the tumultuous years were over and risk of swift death no longer challenged her fierce devotion, did not her natural reticence hold him too much at bay?

They were a wonderfully united family: Jan was a joy to them both, intelligent of heart and mind. He, too, hid emotions too deep for expression. It was his mother rather than his father who held his confidence, for these two understood each other without words. But Waclaw was always his good companion. In spite of the difference of age his father always remained very youthful-looking. The thick black hair turned grey, but his eyes never lost their dark brilliance; his face was quick-moving and arrestingly expressive; he was a tireless skater and walker. Pupils came to him literally from all over the world, and if he tended to discourage Olga's performances in public he turned over much of his teaching to her.

"So-and-so gave a fine account of himself at his concert," he would say with pride, speaking of a student. "He did me great honour!"

"But his flying staccato was mine," Olga reminded him, proud too that her hours of patient work should be crowned publicly.

Warsaw itself grew in stature and interest: a very real renaissance animated the arts. "They grow more sure, our artists; they dare to be true to themselves," said Waclaw, thrilled at this realization of all he had hoped and worked for. Music and drama threw off the

artificial nineteenth-century French tradition and blossomed under the direction of young Poles who drew
their inspiration from native sources. The same was
true of painting and of writing: the finest aspect of nationalism influenced them both, and a lively response
from the public quickened this creative effort.

For one talked and discussed things freely then;
one lived very close to actualities in Warsaw; for a few
years its political cabarets were the wittiest in Europe.

Waclaw became more and more of a public figure.
His passionate concern for his country made him a convincing public speaker on subjects ranging far beyond
his music; people likened him to Paderewski and flocked
to hear him.

His interest in other countries and their policies he
naturally wished to share with Olga.

"Why don't you take one of these trips to Russia that
are being arranged?" he suggested one day. "I'm sure
you'd find it stimulating."

She looked at him incredulously. Had he forgotten
her introduction to that country, what she had suffered
within its borders?

"I wouldn't go to Russia," she declared with emphasis, "if you paid me a million dollars."

It was late in June, 1939, that Olga awoke one night
from a painfully vivid dream. A shot seemed to ring
through the darkness and a bird flew into her room,
a huge winged creature whose claws were dripping
blood. It perched above the lintel of the door, and immediately she had a presentiment of disaster.

"I must go and see what has happened to Waclaw,"
she thought, all the old terrors reviving with the

prompting of her love. She rose to seek him, as the bird flew out of the window.

But she had forgotten her fears as they walked together two evenings later through the park by the Conservatoire. A colleague came to meet them, a piano professor, who was obviously very much agitated.

"My brother-in-law has just died," he said. "It is a terrible blow to my wife, and to all of us. We had no warning . . . no idea he was ill; he went . . . just like that." The man raised his hand despairingly, and hurried away, trying to hide his sorrow.

"Ah, Olga, Olga, life is so short," said Waclaw, visibly moved by what he had just heard. "One moment . . . and then you are gone. It is so hard to go with so much left undone. But how much harder for those who are left alone!" He took her hand and drew her arm through his, pressing it against his side to hold her nearer, as though already consoling her for his loss. The old adoring look blazed in his eyes as he turned to her, mutely pleading for some admission on her part.

He continued to caress her fingers slowly as they walked along in silence.

Before next day dawned his great heart failed him, and he too was dead.

7. WINTER

Winter came early to Zimny Gorodok in 1940. Before the end of August the silver birch trees turned pale yellow and brown, and made little ghostly groves among the forest of dark evergreens. A few gusts of wind tore at the leaves, patterning the coarse grass and matted tangle of undergrowth with their delicate shapes and glistening colour. There was no rain to rot them, so they lay for weeks on the black earth, beautiful and immaculate.

The twilight at dawn and dusk grew ever more long-drawn-out and lovely. Each evening, while the sun glowed golden in the west, the east shimmered in a pale lavender light which dyed the pines and birches and streaked with bright violet bands the sky immediately above them.

Sometimes the whole picture was duplicated in the river and the still water turned gold and amethyst. The air was so limpid that each twig was a vivid line etched delicately distinct from all the others.

Then, as though ashamed of such prodigality of beauty, harsh winter fell, and by the middle of September the first fine snow came tingling down, dry and hard, pricking the eyes and cheeks of the prisoners, who were aghast to see the cold weather come so soon.

None of them were prepared for the alarming drop in the temperature; most of them possessed only the summer clothes in which they had been arrested, and in all lurked an immeasurable fear conjured by the words "Siberian winter."

Waiting in the long queues now was real torture. When the morning gong sounded for them to appear before the *Nachalnik*, they shivered at the very thought of this ordeal. At that early hour some of them had already stood in line to buy bread and the herb mixture they brewed in lieu of tea. If only they had been allowed to buy supplies for several days at a time, or if they could only have been given their work for a week in advance, life would have been less rigorous; but they were forced to live from day to day, and from hand to mouth, that their routine might have its daily quota of sordid misery.

Huddling together before the *Nachalnik's* cabin was out of the question, for the guards were always on duty insisting on a semblance of straight lines. Only very occasionally, when the cold was so intense as to make them break rank themselves, clapping their arms and thighs and stamping their feet, did they close their eyes to any lack of discipline on the part of the prisoners.

Olga desperately turned over the contents of her suitcase, wondering how she could possibly cope with the freezing weather. Her hands and feet, swollen with chilblains, suffered most. Kid gloves and silk stockings, so full of holes and runs they would hardly hold together, were all she had to protect them. She weighed the possibilities of each garment carefully: there was almost nothing in wool but the little knitted top of a sun-bathing suit—she would never need that in camp! Cutting it up and utilizing every scrap and adding the cuffs taken from a sweater she managed to make a pair of mittens and two socks. The leg of the sock was a bit of thin woolen interlining stolen from her coat.

From the coat's fur collar she took just enough to contrive a tiny muff, even adding at each end a flounce of matching material taken from the coat's basque.

"Not only warm, but elegant," she declared, showing the result to Mrs. Altberg. The latter was full of admiration.

"How well you've managed!" she exclaimed. "I would never have believed so little material would go so far."

Olga was elated by her own ingenuity, and even more so when she found that she had, after all, included in her hastily packed bag a pair of cloth-top overshoes. Wearing her woolen socks and blue velvet bed slippers thrust into the overshoes, she felt ready to step out into the snow; and she was the only one in camp who had the luxury of a muff.

All the women did their best to adapt to camp conditions, but how much harder it all was in the bitter cold, with their clothes growing every day more threadbare from their strenuous work. How they grieved over the faithlessness of *things*—the skirts that sagged and split; the sleeves that rubbed through at the elbows; broken shoes that they patched and held together with great stitches, but which finally dropped to pieces and had to be thrown out.

Word went through the camp one day that new shoes would be on sale at the store for those whose work entitled them to a shoe coupon; and many a prisoner, thinking of the bad weather ahead, counted his money carefully, deciding to make a sacrifice of food in order to be adequately shod.

Ignac Stupek was among those who came to buy. The little tailor who had suffered so miserably during the outward journey was almost a stranger in the camp, for as soon as he had recovered from his attack of dysentery he had been transferred to the Lejkin barracks. Now he was back again, still faintly cocky, an indomitable little figure, though he had never achieved his ambition of sewing for the Soviet government, but had been kept hard at work in a sawmill. Armed with his precious purchase permit, he inspected the boots and shoes on sale. It was a typical Soviet bargain: not only were the shoes not new, but there were no pairs. You picked out two as nearly alike as possible, and the price was twenty roubles—actually about a month's salary, if you were a woman; or the equivalent of two weeks' time of a man's work.

Ignac bought himself some oxfords, and though they did not match, he somehow could not refrain from strutting in them a little, just because they were the first objects he had ever bought with money he had earned in camp. Poor Ignac Stupek! Life was one long disappointment for him. He had not worn them three days when the uppers parted company with the soles, and even the soles turned out to be imitation leather.

Some of the women who could afford it and who managed to get permits, bought winter clothes at the store, but they could find nothing really warm. Everything was factory-made. Soviet mass-production had killed all the lovely old Russian hand-loomed materials and finely worked furs, and in a short time their purchases were so faded and tattered that their original shape and shade were barely recognizable. Olga was sometimes horrified to discover that drab figures, whom in the distance she had taken for natives, turned out to be camp colleagues in store garments.

She herself had nothing to face the winter in but a woolen skirt and sweater which she wore every day, together with the faithful coat which served, in addition, as dressing gown, bed cover, and, slung over a rope across the cabin, as room partition as well.

The men's problems were less exacting, as their clothes withstood the ravages of work and weather better than did the women's. They were spared, too, that particular heartache women suffered as the brutal life so relentlessly withered their looks. No longer did they dare look in their mirrors; the gaunt, pallid faces that stared back at them, with coarsened, unwashed hair and ruined skin, brought home to them more than anything else the extent of their misery.

Most of the men grew beards, through lack of razors and soap. But both Mr. Fischer and Dr. Altberg continued to shave. Their spruce appearance had a definitely heartening effect on the others, whatever the cost to themselves; and in the cabin, with the rapidly darkening days, they all stood in need of every bit of added morale visible. Winter's arrival steeped the place in gloom; and the pessimistic doctor particularly had been more than usually depressed and full of foreboding in spite of his clean-shaven cheeks.

He would never survive the exile, he was convinced, as soon as he saw the first snow fall. And if the war lasted long, as he felt quite sure it would, none of them would ever leave Siberia. His wife and daughter were reduced to tears at this fresh outbreak of doleful predictions; and Olga would seize him by the shoulders and try to shake him out of his despondency.

"Now, doctor, doctor, how can you say such things? You know we are all going to be freed one day. How you talk!" Then he would feel a little better and concede that, maybe after all, his wife and Kazia might live to get away, even if his own demise were inevitable.

Yet there was surprisingly little sickness, considering the wretched conditions. The tiny children grew thinner and wilder; they snatched at the black bread and ate voraciously whenever they had the chance, always on the prowl for food. But they flourished like weeds. The twelve- to sixteen-year-olds led a listless, disorganized life. Steputin ordered a ping-pong table for them and tried to start baseball games; but they had little heart for sport; and soon it was entirely too cold to play outdoors.

These adolescents wore the same strained look that stamped the faces of their elders. They were either in a perpetual suppressed rage, or else so dejected that it was impossible for them to give their minds to anything that went on in camp.

Not one of them really believed that he was there for good: at worst it was like a stop-over at some evil inn, on a journey far from home; and since the longing to return was so incessant, they all went around in a kind of waking dream, taciturn and morose, half ashamed of their secret hopings but quite unable to relinquish them.

In this state, with nothing to relieve the monotony of their impressions, their nerves, unduly irritable when provoked, grew gradually more and more apathetic. When one of their number died, they were shocked at their own indifference. Yet Marysia had been their companion for months, a good-hearted girl who, as brigadier among the field labourers, had always tried to hearten them and lighten their work. She herself was from the mountains, sturdy and resourceful, with a real knowledge of agriculture; she could have been invaluable to the Russians with advice on scientific farming, but she had been sent to the dread Lejkin barracks and returned shortly after, as so many had done, broken in health and spirit.

She languished in her cabin, where Dr. Altberg attended her secretly; then she was removed to the dispensary. This was only a shack a little bigger than the other log cabins, and there was little medical care. But she might have recovered had the Soviet authorities not decided, just at that moment, to transform the dispensary building into a nursery and kindergarten. It was high time, they declared, to take the smaller children away from the bourgeois influence of their parents and inoculate them with a few sound Soviet principles. So the patients were literally turned out of doors that the builders might set to work.

Into the bitter cold tottered the sick and the dying.

The unlucky Rabbi's daughter was among them, a victim of pneumonia. Olga was horrified to see her trailing blankets and stumbling through the street, supported by her friends though she could hardly put one foot before the other. She reached her father's cabin where ultimately she recovered, but Marysia was taken to Schabarow, and she never came back.

Poor Marysia, said the prisoners. The first death! But how many more will follow, they questioned dully, shrugging off their sorrow. Actually, most of them suffered only occupational injuries and minor ills: there was a wonderful quality in the air that kept them going in spite of themselves.

Ruptures were common. Men and women suffered alike, for they were too unprepared and ill-equipped for the heavy work; toothache plagued them and most of them lost the fillings from their teeth owing to the insufficient, unbalanced diet; their sight dimmed, and they had headaches; yellow purulent sores broke out everywhere on their skin, yet the dull, grinding round never ceased. Unless they had more than 101 degrees of fever work was never excused: the *feldsher*—that characteristic Russian institution of half-trained doctor for village practice—was adamant on this score. Not that fever itself was treated as anything very serious; the Soviet authorities obviously expected their Polish patients to exhibit the stolid endurance of Siberian peasants.

When the *feldsher* was visiting a neighbouring village and his assistant lanced a boil for the Rabbi's son-in-law, blood-poisoning set in, his arm swelled to alarming proportions and his fever raged. Yet in this condition, and quite alone, he had to walk the five miles into Schabarow for treatment. An epileptic, who fell down in a fit and broke his hand, was not given even one day's convalescence, for in spite of the great pain and his inability to use his hand, his fever never rose above a hundred.

What the camp chiefly lacked were simple home remedies. Olga was the proud possessor of a bottle of mercurochrome, and more people turned to her for assistance than to the *feldsher* or to any of the medical men in the camp. Dr. Altberg had telegraphed to Lemberg for supplies of drugs, urging that they be flown to him immediately; but nothing ever arrived, and he could not fill his prescriptions; so most of the cuts and burns and poisoned fingers were treated by "Dr." Olga, who had the satisfaction of curing more than one nasty-looking wound that might have proved fatal.

A curious phenomenon was that from the very first all the women ceased menstruating. Whether this was due to the diet or shock of arrest and hard labour they did not know, and none cared to discuss the matter with the *feldsher*. Though it puzzled them, most regarded it as a merciful dispensation of Providence, for the general store carried nothing for their needs. Half the time even toilet paper was not available; and now that the summer foliage was gone and the latrines frozen hard and unusable (for they had all been dug too shallow) there were various other problems of an intimate and disagreeable nature that nevertheless had to be faced every day and night.

How winter increased the misery and burden of their work! Even the daily fetching of water became a serious matter, for the hill to the well was a sheet of ice. Olga and Kazia, setting out with a pail on a stick between them, tried to laugh off the situation by likening themselves to Jack and Jill. Whenever possible, they carried ashes to strew on the slope, but even then the descent was perilous with a full pail. Both took many a spill; until at last the well itself froze solid and their trials were over, for now the snow was deep and they could fill a pail outside their door and melt it over the stove.

Much of Olga's work during their first cold weeks consisted of hauling and carrying, for the field work ceased. The men in the carpenter's shop had been struggling to prepare double window frames for the cabins. Numbed with the cold and hampered by lack of tools, they had been at it for weeks, but no glass panes could be had and they had become discouraged and whittled aimlessly away at the wood. Vast amounts of sawdust lay around the place and Olga was ordered to collect all this and take it to the men engaged in putting up a bathhouse near the jetty. They used it for insulation between two plank walls. Naturally, there was no receptacle for handling the stuff and she was forced to make a rough hod which was no easy object to carry so far. Back and forth, back and forth, for a distance of several blocks, fifty times a day she plodded, her hands growing more and more numbed, her back aching with the awkward load. But at least she knew there was some purpose in the work; the builders needed that sawdust. What she resented most, and what tried her strength beyond endurance, was the complete uselessness which characterized so much of what she was given to do.

How many times had she dragged lumpy sacks of potatoes from one cellar to another, only to spade them up again and carry them elsewhere! Emptying kerosene from one great tank into another kept her busy one day for more than twelve long hours; it was a torment, an insult to intelligence; nothing brought home to her so much her own abject position, which permitted such humiliation and callous disregard. But there was no getting out of the order.

"All this must be emptied before nightfall," commanded the *Nachalnik*, assigning five other women to work with her; and when the morning work gong sounded her labour gang set out.

With clumsy wooden dippers to fill the heavy pails, they began making the senseless transfer. Maria Wysocki was among the workers and she was quick to suggest that at least they provide themselves with some of the precious fluid. It was so expensive and their daily ration so small that they never had enough to light their cabins; and above all they prized it for destroying lice. But the guard kept very strict watch on them, refusing to allow any personal profit from their labour.

"Not a drop," he declared when they begged him to let them fill just one small bottle to take home. "Not a single drop!" Yet before they had finished their exhausting task, quarts had been spilled and wasted as they ladled out the slowly diminishing bulk.

Eight weary miles they must have walked in all, carrying the pails between them; one hundred and twenty times they strained to dip and empty the greasy, stinking loads; and their wrath and resentment smouldered and blazed when they saw that the tank they were filling leaked. Everything above the crack in its side seeped out and was lost, making a double mockery of their dire need and the back-breaking imposition.

Daylight had long since vanished before the last pail was emptied, and the women were dropping from fatigue. Dr. Altberg was alarmed at Olga's prolonged absence. "But what can be keeping her all this time?" he demanded a hundred times, storming round the camp, his fertile imagination foreseeing a dozen horrible calamities. He waited by the tanks till the guard finally released the workers, ready to help her back to the cabin, where she collapsed on her bed crying helplessly with exhaustion as Mrs. Altberg and Kazia scurried in the dark to get her something to eat.

Yet, next morning, with scrupulous Soviet irony, the six women were paid for working overtime, and granted, moreover, the privilege of purchasing with this pittance a gill of olive oil. This was so rare a luxury that there was a general celebration in the cabin. Olga was toasted in herb tea, for instead of the daily boiled ration, they luxuriated in French-fried potatoes.

Their lives were so bleak that they welcomed the slightest variation as an occasion to rally their spirits; time would have seemed endless had they overlooked such moments of simple pleasure.

Kazia's sixteenth birthday was approaching and Mrs. Altberg and Olga racked their brains for a fitting birthday party. They stinted on bread to buy a little flour, and hunted around under the snow for the red whortleberries which still lingered on. These rattled like bullets on the hard earth and their tart pungent flavour puckered the mouth. Though the prisoners sometimes cooked them with the sickly sweet frozen potatoes, making a mush to spread on bread, no one was able to take full advantage of this inexhaustible supply of fruit.

But Mrs. Altberg took from a hidden supply a little of her precious sugar and made jam and spread it on the cake that she had baked. Olga decorated the cabin with pine branches; and the Fischers and Brombergs were invited to the feast.

In they all came after the day's work was over—serfs and outcasts who found again the courage to be themselves. The cabin was practically in darkness, deep shadows filled every corner, but round the bench where they gathered were light and determined happiness. A slender wick burned in a tiny bottle of kerosene, and by its glow Kazia cut her birthday cake and gave them all a slice. They held it carefully in their hands, mindful of every crumb; eating it slowly, savouring each mouthful of the sticky, luscious treat. They laughed and licked their fingers; and then the young people played games, forgetting for the moment they were in Siberia; and they all sang songs—lusty Polish songs with the men's voices drowning the trebles; and other songs that were softer and not so gay. Mr. Fischer played his xylophone, accompanying the Imp's bird-like soprano. Last of all they sang their national anthem, humming it very quietly at first, for this was strictly forbidden—a punishable offence. But their defiance rose with the melody; it was exciting to risk detection. And before they separated they sang it several times beneath their breath.

Camp life was poisoned by constant little fears at the prospect of punishment for petty offenses; one was never free from a feeling of guilt. The least deviation from the ordered round meant swift retribution. If discovered, fines, solitary confinement, or exile to the terrible Lejkin or Schabarow barracks would be their lot; yet, when they really decided to break the rules, nothing deterred them.

When Olga found that her mattress needed refilling, she and a neighbour went out to steal hay. They carried her rug, and in the dark, after work hours, dug into one of the stacks near the forest, cutting deep into the middle to get it good and dry. They piled the rug high, not pausing to thin out the brambles and thistles; but carrying it home, they saw two guards approaching and, horrified, began to run in the opposite direction. They dared not drop their cumbersome load, and dared not go straight back to the cabin. Chased over fields and ditches by the men, stumbling over fences with their great bundle between them, barking their shins, and with their hands scratched and torn, they finally reached home, furious with themselves for being so afraid. They decided that the game was not worth the candle, and were ready to abide by the rules in the future.

Yet they risked official anger again when they outwitted the delousing commission which was scheduled to clean the cabins. In spite of all their efforts, many of them could not keep free from lice; those who came back from the barracks always found their clothes infested. The Soviet authorities took a very serious view of this, bitterly reproaching the prisoners for such a state, at the same time making the purchase of soap and kerosene practically prohibitive. They brutally shaved the head of one poor girl—the lonely child who had been found at a roadside station on the journey to camp. "Black Beauty," the camp had nicknamed her for the masses of heavy curls that hung below her waist, a shining, incomparable glory.

She had never got rid of the pests that she had picked up sleeping in the dirty railway station; her roommates did all they could to help her, trying everything they had, patiently combing through the lustrous mantle of hair. When she applied to the dispensary for a remedy, Steputin's wife cut it all off and burnt it. It was as if she had struck at the girl's life: she drooped and pined, her naked head grotesque above her dark, mournful eyes, some vital spring quenched in her.

Drastic measures against lice, warned the authorities, would be taken throughout the entire camp; and prisoners were told that everything they possessed must pass through the delousing machines.

"And can you imagine what they will look like when they come out with everything mashed together?" grumbled Olga, as the cabin met in discussion over the new edict.

"My fine *breitschwanze* coat!" moaned Mrs. Altberg.

"And mine!" echoed Mrs. Fischer.

"Well, don't give them up; just say they are not

verminous and do not have to be disinfected," suggested Henryk. "Stick to them! Be firm!"

The women looked at each other doubtfully. Just what chance would they have of being firm when guards came to collect their property.

"Well then, hide them," went on Henryk, when he realized his other proposition met with no approval.

But where could anything be hid? There was not an inch in the cabin that was not immediately visible on entrance.

After much deliberation they decided on the woodpile; the great mass of sawed logs from which the prisoners drew their weekly ration. Late that night they stole out to secrete their belongings, not without much trepidation, for everything would surely have been confiscated if discovered. Dr. Altberg and Olga kept watch while Henryk helped Mr. Fischer and his wife as they lifted and tugged and finally managed to push the coats, and a few other objects, into the midst of the logs, well out of sight.

Two or three days passed while, as often as they could, the cabin occupants hovered, like squirrels watching a nut, in the neighbourhood of the woodpile.

When all danger of delousing was over, they set out to recover their property, but that proved very much harder than hiding it. A lot of the wood had slipped, and the coats were much more effectively hidden from sight than their owners bargained for. With hearts quaking at every sound, they pushed and pulled, fearful of tearing the fur in the dark, afraid of being caught, shivering with cold and the unwonted exertion, and consumed with that constant resentment that they should be forced into such ignominious situations. It was an hour before they returned to the cabin, worn out and half frozen, but elated that they had got the best of the commission and kept their possessions intact.

The prisoners had been standing an hour in the rising wind, waiting for their daily meal. Snow was beginning to fall again, whipped into flurries by the driving gusts. It stung their faces with spiteful force as they lowered their heads, drawing their scarves and shawls tighter about them, thin shoulders cowering against the storm. Slowly the long line advanced toward the cook shed; a few at a time they pressed inside, avid for the hot soup, breathing with difficulty, dazed, their hair and eyelids dripping as the hard snow gradually unfroze in the steamy warmth.

There was a new face behind the counter where they presented their work cards for the check-up. A young Polish woman replaced the dour Soviet official who usually handed out the rations. How was it, everyone asked, that an exile had been assigned such an easy job? To be indoors all day near a stove, while others worked in the cold, was unusually good fortune, especially for someone obviously qualified for hard labour.

Anna, the new serving-woman, was a plump, pleasing-looking creature with reddish-blonde hair, and a broad, flat nose, more like a Russian in appearance than the rest of her compatriots. Her husband had recently been removed to Lejkin, and no sooner had he disappeared than Anna had stepped into her comfortable position.

Gossip was unusual in the camp: there was neither the inclination nor opportunity for much exchange of small talk. Prisoners visited each other rarely and kept pretty much to their cabin mates. Camp solidarity, too, would ordinarily have restrained any inclination to malice, but Anna's job set tongues wagging. Why should she be treated so much better than all the others? they demanded. And the question rankled the more they shivered.

Shortly afterwards a guard entered the shed while the breadline waited. Anna's face flamed as he stood at her side, watching her movements. The prisoners could not help noting her blushes and embarrassment; she fumbled their cards in her confusion at the guard's presence; she dropped a plate in sheer nervousness when he came nearer; and their amusement increased when they looked at her escort.

It was Kurkof, the pock-marked simpleton, who stood there so proud and complacent, both hands on his hips, his peasant face broadened in a grin of unabashed satisfaction; Kurkof, who was flattered when the prisoners called him "mister," who had been so bewildered at first by the arrival of "all these fine people" and whose hesitations as a guard could usually be exploited by the Poles to their own advantage. *Pan* Kurkof a lover!

So that was how the land lay.

Let Anna keep her job if Kurkof went with it! Rancour evaporated as the news spread, and a tolerant indifference took its place.

Whatever the prisoners held against the Russians, no woman could complain that she was ever molested in camp. Behaviour on this score was more than correct.

Olga had once seen a guard kissing two schoolgirls; but they were such unhappy-looking, frightened children that the gesture had anything but the appearance of an assault.

Indeed, the frigidity and solitude of the region seemed to affect the lives of all its inhabitants. With the enforced promiscuity of a camp this size, the very opposite might have been imagined; but sexual desire seemed to have died with their hopes. Lack of opportunity no doubt played a part in this sexless existence; with eight people to a cabin and guards on duty everywhere, seclusion was well-nigh impossible.

One of the accountants, it was whispered, occasionally solicited women when he paid them their wages. He had a lecherous face, red as a crab, with thin grey hair, mean little eyes and nervous hands always tugging at his drooping moustache. "Old Two-eggs," the Poles called him, for he offered, so they said, two eggs to any woman who would lie with him. One of the prisoners was known to have accepted his proposals, but she herself was so worn and old, her complaisance had all the aspects of a sacrifice.

"Some child's health may depend on those eggs," said the other prisoners, with a charitable understanding of infinite degradation.

Only one romance flourished in the colony, a brief love affair which ended in marriage between the Hollywood Girl and the Communist.

She did not come from Hollywood, of course; she was a student from the Warsaw School of Drama, a strikingly beautiful Jewess whose plucked eyebrows and general allure won her this nickname. She had been arrested in the country outside Lemberg and had only slacks and pyjamas with her; no one ever saw her working in anything else; and very well she looked in them too.

The camp did not know if her young man was really a Communist or not. Like everyone else who has seen the "Peoples' Government" in action on the spot, he had probably lost his convictions at the first contact—if indeed he had ever had any—but he was always referred to by this title, however.

The attachment of the two young people dated from the terrible train journey which they had made together; and either by request or accident they had been assigned the same cabin. So they asked the Soviet authorities to marry them, and although the wedding ceremony was a most perfunctory affair, like stamping a bread card and all over in a minute, their continued happiness was the greatest satisfaction to the rest, who were delighted that one spark of love could exist in the midst of such wholesale dreariness.

For unhappiness had not made the exiles either bitter or spiteful; they felt rather a deep sense of union and more kindliness than would have been generated under normal circumstances. Whenever one of their number was punished or exiled to other barracks they always took up a subscription for dependents left behind. Out of their pitiful wages they gave a few kopeks to the ones who could earn nothing: though their constant fear was finding themselves unable to buy even the meagre ration that stood between themselves and star-

vation, they never refused such an appeal. One or two
Poles had considerable sums of hidden money, and
their generosity was well known; and many others
found means to help less fortunate companions. The
British war veteran mended watches for his fellow prisoners and was glad to earn extra money for his ailing
son; Olga gave English lessons to three students in her
few spare hours, and this not only eked out her wages
but was tangible, resonant proof of her independence,
and one of her greatest consolations, now that real liberty had vanished.

How much she depended on those around her, what
comfort she drew from their warm-hearted support,
she never fully realized until a terrible fate threatened
to sweep it all from her.

She was returning to her cabin from the carpenters'
shop one evening when a familiar figure loomed out of
the darkness and came towards her. It was the Polish
brigadier, the man with the passion for music. He took
her arm and without a word walked her beyond the
limit of the cabins and towards the forest. He neither
whistled nor sang as he always used to, and Olga wondered at his action and his silence. When they had gone
a long way and could not possibly be seen or followed,
he turned to her.

"*Pani* Kochanska, I have something to tell you," he
began. She looked at him wonderingly. "I am escorting
a group of prisoners to Lejkin tomorrow and may not
be back again for a long time."

Olga caught his hand in quick sympathy.

"You are going to that dreadful place!" she said

compassionately. "And those poor, poor creatures who have to go with you!"

He looked at her again, swallowing hard, almost unable to speak.

"*Pani* Kochanska," he whispered, "your name is on the list too."

"No!" she shrieked. "No! I cannot bear it. Why am I being sent? What have I done? I cannot go! I simply cannot face life there alone."

She turned from him, her face hidden in her hands, her shoulders heaving; for the first time he saw her bowed like an old woman, her courage broken.

He shifted about uneasily, not knowing what to do. "She wouldn't be alone," he thought. "I should be there and could probably make things a little easier for her. . . ." But her silent anguish moved him far more than he could have imagined. He hated to have any part in her banishment, though the fault was certainly not his. And he was racked by his memories of the dazzling figure he had once seen on a concert platform and the pitiful spectacle now before him; torn by his desire to help her and the sense of his own powerlessness. He kicked at the snow as she cried silently.

"Listen," he said finally, "we are not going till tomorrow. When the work gong sounds, don't go near the *Nachalnik*. I have to call out the names and take my lot with me. I shall simply miss yours out. I'm responsible for those who go, and the Bolshies will probably be too slack to check over the list themselves. If they do, I can easily say I made a slip; but if you're not around they will most likely have forgotten that you were included. It isn't as if yours were a prison sentence . . . it's a simple transfer this time."

Now that he had made a decision and had a plan of action his awkwardness vanished. He recovered his confidence. "It will be all right," he said, patting her arm consolingly. "I'm sure it will be quite simple. You stay on here . . . among your friends; they will take care of you."

Olga gulped down her tears. "I don't know how to thank you," she said gratefully. "You are all so good to me."

"No thanks needed," he said gruffly. They were coming back to the cabins. "I shall not be seeing you for a long time, I suppose," he said slowly, "so I'll say goodbye. . . . I wish you every possible good luck, *pani* Kochanska." He shook her hand, a very powerful, hard handshake, and then she left him.

The man continued his way along the white path that stretched between the log buildings. Though all the prisoners were home from work, hardly a light showed in the windows or between the cracks of the doors. It was like a deserted village.

A silver crescent sailed out of the clouds, picking out the pointed tops of the roofs and the little glass panes covered with ice. There was no sound at all except the crunching of dry light snow beneath the man's boots. He gazed up at the moon for a long while, and as he walked slowly in the direction of his own cabin he began to whistle a Bach concerto.

8. THE ARRIVAL

"IF you took my penknife
and hacked it a bit . . ."
said Olga.

"Or if you used the piece of tin I scrape the floor
with . . ." volunteered the Imp.

"Perhaps you should breathe hard and try melting
it. . . ."

Suggestions were not lacking as the cabin occupants
watched the doctor at his labours.

They were discussing the heavy layer of ice that
coated the inside windowpane. It was almost an inch
thick, and even after the sun melted the ice outside,
it clung to the glass, obscuring the light and adding
considerably to the cold in the cabin.

Dr. Altberg was doing his best to scrape it away, yet
this seemingly simple task was proving too much for
him. His fingers ached as he worked over the stubborn
mass, and he made hardly more than a slight impression on the edge of it.

It annoyed and depressed him beyond measure that
he was unable to deal with such an everyday matter.
"Surely," he felt, "I could have adapted by this time to

the primitive conditions under which I am forced to live!" But such was not the case. Samuel Altberg, who could perform operations demanding the most meticulous precision, and whose patience was unfailing in the diagnosis of intricate and obscure symptoms, found himself completely exhausted when called upon to do a little housework.

And his immediate recognition of this fact merely increased his ill-humour.

Yet it was Dr. Altberg who complained most of the darkness in which they now lived, and who insisted on this frenzied attack upon the windowpane.

There was no light in the sky until about nine in the morning; and not until the sun was high in the heavens did a little filter through the ice-cap on the window into the cabin.

"It's like an opal," said Olga, standing by the doctor's side and watching the effect of the rays as they splintered on its gleaming surface. "It's like a great fire-opal."

"How can you say such things?" he demanded. "How can you possibly admire anything under these circumstances?"

He himself was incapable of ecstasy at nature's miracles, yet as he turned on her almost angrily, he was ashamed when he saw her complete absorption in this detail of fragile beauty. Her great almond-shaped eyes seemed to be drinking in the colour, her lips parted like a child's; and her thin sad face was lit with wonder. Such rapt longing, the doctor considered, was entirely wasted upon abstract delight.

She must have felt the intensity of his regard, for she came back to herself with a little sigh.

"Now you leave that window alone," she said, drawing him away. "You've worked long enough over it, and the sun will melt it in time anyway."

He allowed her to persuade him to do exactly what he had intended doing, reflecting grimly that the sun would indeed not be long in sending a trickle of water down the wall under the window. It would snake dankly across the floor until it joined the puddle near the door.

Great shards of ice jutted from the door jamb every night and morning: Olga had packed it as tightly as she could with moss, using the same grey weather-stripping to stop the cracks round the window, but nothing seemed to keep at bay the penetrating cold. The fire burned in the stove each night and morning, a goodly supply of wood was stacked in the passage between the two rooms, but this did little more than melt the ice and make a cloud of steam in the cabin. The ceiling dripped; dampness oozed from the clay in the floor; and as darkness fell about three o'clock everything froze hard again. When Olga crept into her bed at night and noted the blanket of ice that covered the inside walls for a distance of three feet above the ground, she had the impression of getting into a tray in an ice box.

Nights were terrible. No one slept well: they huddled, cramped and aching, under their thin covers. They got up each morning in the dark, and when work was over the cabin was again in darkness. Their supply of kerosene was so meagre they could never use the big lamp hanging in the middle of the ceiling, and dared not always light the tiny wick stuck in a medicine bottle; when they wanted to find their way around the room before going to bed, they burned a pine knot on the stove. It sputtered and blazed, filling the place with smoke and fitful shadows until—about ten minutes after —it sank in ashes. They coughed and gasped, worrying a little about the black smudges the smoke left on the plaster. Three times during the winter they had freshened their walls and ceiling, digging deep for grey clay near the river and mixing it gingerly with melted snow before they spread it with their hands. But the effect never lasted long; the camp inspector railed continually at the sooty interior, and with equal obstinacy they continued to employ their flaming torches whenever they needed them.

Today they sat in the cabin, busy with their own affairs. It was not Sunday but the thermometer had dropped to thirty-five degrees below zero, and at that temperature camp work ceased; not from any humane point of view, but simply because it was too difficult to keep large numbers of prisoners employed now that field work was no longer possible. The carpenters' shop and building sheds were all unheated; hands became so numbed that work was slowed up till it hardly paid the authorities to keep so many on the job, and 35° was a handy measure at which to call a halt.

Actually, it made very little difference whether it was 25° or 35° below. Peasants used to leave their cows out at night when it was as low as 50°, with only an occasional fence to shelter them from snowdrifts. Once winter fell and it froze in Siberia, it stayed frozen. The air was so dry and, except when it was snowing, so utterly still, that the prisoners found that in spite of their great sufferings, the climate did not kill them. In a damper country, even with much less cold but subject to wind and sudden changes, they would probably all have died with the little they had to heat and clothe them.

In Zimny Gorodok it was generally too cold to snow, and at the worst there was scarcely eighteen inches under foot; yet colds were unknown, for germs could not survive in that atmosphere.

The cabin was hardly a comfortable place to sit in, but a day of leisure was a very welcome respite.

"And now I should think you could do something about your skirt, *pani* Kochanska," remarked Mrs. Altberg, as Olga and Dr. Altberg turned from their exertions on the windowpane.

"Why, what's the matter with my skirt?" asked Olga.

"Nothing much, except that the back of it is just about out," remarked Mrs. Altberg dryly.

"You see what comes from dressing and undressing in the dark," sighed Olga, "I had no idea what was going on behind my back."

She examined it ruefully, measuring and calculating how much she could take from the sides or hem to reinforce the worn part; she had almost no thread left . . . no one in camp had any thread, and there had been none on sale for weeks. She fitted and sewed, working clumsily with her chilblained fingers, straining her eyes in the dim light.

How long would the skirt last? she wondered. And what would happen when she could really no longer hold it together? Her silk and cotton dresses seemed a mockery in this frigid climate; yet she could never put aside enough money to buy anything new. Her camp work brought her in hardly twenty roubles a month; much less, of course, than what she was entitled to or had been promised, but it was useless to protest to the accountant on that score. He would find a dozen arguments to prove that she could get no more in cash, whatever elaborate arrangements of "credit" he might make. Even with her English lessons she did not earn enough to meet the price of cotton goods asked in the store.

She began to get panicky when she thought of the long winter before her: it was not yet the end of November and there would be no change in the weather till May. How could she possibly get through those months with what she had to wear? Her food ration was hardly above starvation level, she dared not save on that.

Chances of release seemed as far off as ever. A letter from Madame Ostrowska, indeed, had started fresh misgivings, for it told of the recent arrival of a notice from the Moscow Embassy, addressed to her at Lemberg! Were the Americans then still ignorant of the fact that she had been arrested? Had nothing reached them telling of her plight? When he left for Lejkin, her friend the Polish brigadier promised to send a telegram to Madame Ostrowska, asking her to wire Moscow. But perhaps the mail left as irregularly from Lejkin as it obviously did from the camp.

Her sewing dropped in her hands as her mind went racing over the future. And Jan? If he were alive, would he get news of her? Was it possible, in the turmoil that was Poland, for him to trace where she had gone?

What must he be suffering, if he had really survived, to come back and find his mother's name among the missing?

She bent her head to hide the tears that gathered in her eyes. If only she could stop thinking! If only she could keep to the plodding monotony of perpetual work and shut out these fearful possibilities that assailed every moment of her leisure!

She glanced up at the window, trying to recapture her mood at the sight of the ice opal, but in vain. The great jewel had vanished, and water drippled in its place.

"But at least the sun has come through at last," she thought, her mouth set in a determined line as she turned again to her sewing.

Kazia was busy making a box out of cardboard and coloured string. She had found balls of bright twine in the store and collected bits of cardboard like a magpie. Now she was working diligently, her clever fingers fashioning little trays to fit into a workbox for her mother. Dr. Altberg sat by the stove, reading for the third or fourth time a copy of *Pravda* which Mr. Meyer, a camp colleague, had loaned him. It was only recently that a newspaper had arrived in Zimny Gorodok. This single copy of the official Russian mouthpiece came from Lemberg, where Meyer had subscribed to it for years. The Soviet authorities had been highly suspicious, however, when it had first been forwarded to him in camp and had confiscated it. Now they had become reconciled to its regular appearance and relaxed their severity.

Dr. Altberg's reaction to a newspaper had been over-whelming for him. For the first time in more than four months his eyes fastened on the printed word. After the vacuity of that awful interim, he was so shaken with emotion he could hardly hold the paper steady enough to read. He devoured the contents, avid for the news but racked by memories which it evoked. All his past life rose before him; all the activities that filled his time when, instead of an animal existence, he led the life of a man; his responsibilities and satisfactions surged up in mockery as he plunged into an account of what was going on in the world outside the prison.

No one ever guessed what insidious torture the reading was . . . nor how he relished it. Like a man probing an aching tooth the better to savour his pain, he lingered over each copy. The weekly reading was no longer quite so poignant as that first number had been, but he still managed to extract a great deal of suffering from it.

The actual news he very largely discounted. One cannot live in daily contact with the Bolsheviks and believe much of what they print or say; Dr. Altberg had seen what had happened to the Lemberg papers immediately after the Russian invasion, and how the press, like every other function, had been twisted to serve political ends; but he found the news columns very stimulating and they furnished him with endless material for speculation and discussion with Josef Fischer.

Olga was the only other person in the cabin who

could read Russian, but she did little more than glance at the headlines to see if there was any mention of the U. S. A.

"Is America doing anything about the war? Will she send war material to the allied powers?" the exiles always asked her, and she found herself fighting down a feeling of guilt when she was forced to admit that her country was still doggedly neutral, and still bound by the Johnson Act to send nothing to belligerents.

She hated to disappoint them: it was so pitifully obvious that they all looked to America for salvation; they considered that country their only hope, just as much as she did herself. It was the one bright spot on their horizon, yet never, by word or look, did their attitude suggest reproach.

"It would be dreadful if political differences added to our sorrows," Mrs. Altberg had once remarked, partly to reassure Olga about their feelings toward her country, and partly to cover her own indifference to world affairs.

She was a patient, kindly woman, very unassuming and infinitely concerned about her fractious husband. She had been a medical student, and in their early days had worked beside him in the laboratory and consulting room. When he became such an eminent figure in his profession she had withdrawn and devoted her life to surrounding him with every possible care and comfort. She sometimes talked to Olga, a little wistfully, of the flowers she used to cultivate in their lovely home, of the collection of Persian rugs they had assembled with so much interest, and of the annual trip to Vienna they always made together when, for a whole month free from exacting patients, they enjoyed the opera and symphony concerts that meant so much to them both.

Even under the harsh camp conditions she managed to spare her husband as much as possible, trying to avoid annoyances and prepare him little treats. She got up at night to light the stove to heat water for him when he was ill or could not sleep; and when a parcel of food arrived from relatives in Lemberg, she saw to it that he received the best, sharing the rest with Kazia and Olga.

What rejoicing there was when the postman brought a parcel. Those who skimped themselves in Lemberg to send the precious food would have felt more than repaid for their generosity could they have seen what it meant to the half-famished prisoners. There was always a chance that parcels would be withheld, and distribution caused many anxious moments. Mr. Meyer, who received from his three children three tiny packages, was forced to give them up. Such abundance, argued the authorities as they made the confiscation, could only indicate an intention on his part to speculate!

More than anything else they craved candy. It amounted at times to an obsession. They would talk about all the occasions in the past in which they had had opportunities to eat candy and had not done so, and try to explain this extraordinary phenomenon. Their rations included practically no sugar; only twice in four months had it been served them, and now the piercing cold made their longings increasingly urgent. Mrs. Altberg had received that week a package of honeydrops, squashed to a shapeless mass in transit, yet none the less welcome. She had made them last as long as possible, carefully boiling the paper in which they arrived and straining it so that not a scrap of the precious sweetness might be wasted.

There had been half a pound of butter in the parcel too, rancid by the time it reached them, but such a rare luxury that they did not mind in what state it was. Now she was baking potatoes, and soon a comforting smell began to fill the cabin. Mrs. Altberg put the remains of yesterday's bread on the top of the stove as well: it always froze hard and hurt their teeth to eat it, but today there would be butter to moisten the unsavoury mass. No soup, of course—that they were only entitled to buy when they had done a day's work; but potatoes that were not frozen and could be roasted they did not often get, and they were thankful that they had received them on a day when there was time to cook and eat them in comfort.

Olga put her sewing down and placed four battered plates on the bench. Everyone was aware that the potatoes were nearly ready and was watching the proceedings round the stove with deepening interest. It was the great moment of the day, the only one that took their minds off everything else.

Dr. Altberg laid aside his paper and rocked restlessly in his chair, his eyes gimleting the little brown objects on the stove top; Kazia hopped around helping her mother, measuring the butter with a piece of twine to determine exactly how much could be eaten at a sitting. She did not try to hide her delight at the prospect of the feast; the others, after a shamefaced attempt at restraint, gave themselves up to the animal longing for food. They were wolfishly hungry; they crept nearer the stove, their nostrils dilated, their whole being intent on what they were going to eat.

When Mrs. Altberg put the potatoes on their plates it was difficult for them not to grab and cram the food into their mouths. They ate in silence, with terrific concentration, each mouthful chewed again and again to make it last as long as possible. Nothing else mattered at that moment; nothing could touch them. They were hungry and now they were eating: life was as simple as that.

Gradually the tension relaxed as the cruellest pangs were stilled. They emerged from their coma and smiled at each other with satisfaction.

"There is no finer dish in all the world than roast potatoes with butter," said Dr. Altberg, as capricious a gourmet as ever lived in Poland.

"If I ate nothing else to my dying day, I would be content," said Olga.

Next morning there was fog over the river; the temperature rose a degree or so and the prisoners went back to work. It was a grey day with a glint of steel in the atmosphere; the snow looked almost black under the trees.

Since eight in the morning Olga had been working in a cellar under the cook shed. It was just a great hole in the ground, shored up with heavy struts and almost completely filled with potatoes. A couple of planks set edgewise down the middle were supposed to keep a runway in the midst of the supplies, but they had slipped and there was hardly room to move.

"The wicked waste! The wicked waste!" she kept repeating under her breath. It was her job to sort out those potatoes which were really too hard to be eatable and to bring some order into the tumbled mass; and as she looked at the state they were in, and saw the marks of the spade on so many of them, she was shocked and furious at the wanton damage done to this mountain of food.

Earth coated her hands and arms as she plunged again and again into it, hardly knowing where to begin the dreary task. Some of the potatoes were no bigger than chestnuts and felt like pebbles. Why had they been stored with the rest? she wondered. And why, with the acres of good black earth she herself had often tilled, did not the country produce better potatoes anyway?

"It's richer than Illinois dirt, and look what they do with it!" she thought contemptuously. She kicked the board with annoyance and a great load of potatoes came slithering down, almost burying her. She scrambled out of the way, hauling herself up by one of the struts. Now she was on top of the mass, and how could she get the runway clear? The more she scrambled and sorted, the more potatoes came down on top of her; it was the work of Sisyphus. She struggled and bent, and lifted armfuls at a time, but as the dinner gong sounded she realized that she had made no impression on the cellar at all.

"That's probably why I am sent here," she reflected bitterly.

She thrust her numbed, earth-caked hands into her muff and started for the breadline. The chill of the vault had penetrated her bones; even the frosty atmosphere outside was a relief after the dank gloom.

She waited her turn listlessly, too weary to try to push ahead. The line stretched like a shabby snake. On each side, at regular intervals, and at a distance of three feet from the prisoners, guards, in their long fur coats lined with heavy lamb's wool, stood watching, fur caps pulled low over their ears, feet planted wide apart, revolvers stuck in their holsters.

Someone was coming out of the cook shed, calling to her.

"*Pani* Kochanska! *Pani* Kochanska!" There was a tremendous commotion around the entrance and several people left the line and came running towards her.

"It's here!" they shouted, crowding about her. "Your passport has come!"

She put her hand before her eyes, her head throbbing wildly. She could hardly believe what she heard, yet everyone seemed so sure and was calling so delightedly to her.

"Where?" she asked weakly. "Where is it?"

The girl who had first called pushed her way through the crowd and caught Olga's hand.

"My brother saw it at Schabarow," she said triumphantly. "It came by post this morning. It's in a big envelope with the American Embassy seal on it. It's thick enough for a passport. That's surely it, all right."

It was Bronia Minsk who spoke. Her brother was often used as interpreter in the camp, and early that morning he had taken a group of prisoners over to Schabarow.

Everyone was talking excitedly, offering congratulations, and the guards made no attempt to keep any order at all. They looked at the scene with interest as the prisoners crowded about Olga, the women hugging and kissing her, the men wringing her by the hand, all as happy apparently as if her good luck were their own.

"You're the bird that is going to fly out of the cage," exclaimed Mr. Hind kindly, as he and his wife came up to join her.

"I always said you had a ninety-nine per cent chance of getting out!" said Harry Spiro, beaming and looking handsomer than ever. "A ninety-nine per cent chance. I should have said a hundred!" He shook her hand warmly, then turned away suddenly, unable to say any more.

"I wish you'd take me in your suitcase," called out Icek, hopping up and down and almost bursting out of his rags in his excitement. "I wish I could go with you. Tell me, will they send an aeroplane for you? Will you travel by aeroplane? Now you won't have to do any work! You don't need to work any more. Say, I wish I could go with you. Can't you take me along?"

His words found an echo in every heart. Icek always said exactly what everyone else felt. But there was no envy in any of the faces that pressed about her.

"Maybe you'll come back and visit us?" someone suggested, and they all laughed loudly at the idea of an American visiting a Siberian prison camp.

"I'd give half my life for an American passport," said one young man. It was the Communist, and he and his wife stood staring at Olga as if she belonged to another world. ". . . Half my life," he repeated soberly. "I'm glad you've got it at last. You don't know how lucky you are."

Dr. Altberg and his wife had only just heard the great news and came running from their cabin. Mrs. Altberg threw her arms round her friend's neck.

"It's too wonderful. I am so glad, dear," she said, more effusive than Olga had ever seen her before. "You have been so patient. Now I hope you can get away as quickly as possible."

Dr. Altberg did not echo his wife's words, but he caught Olga's hand and pressed it in his. "We shall all miss you here very much; the camp won't be the same without you. But I'm glad, glad that it's come at last."

They stayed with her until she had got her plate of soup and walked back with her to the cabin.

She was so excited she could hardly eat, and her legs shook so that she had to sit down. Now that the passport was actually within her grasp she felt her strength collapsing. She sat there weakly, crying a little, breaking her bread into small pieces.

"When do you think it will get there?" she asked.

"When they deliver the next post," said Dr. Altberg. "I doubt if they send it over expressly, so don't count on it. Mail is usually delivered on Thursday or Friday, so you have two or three days to contain your impatience. But it's better to expect it that way than having any disappointment."

He was quite right, and Olga was grateful for his advice, in spite of his pessimism. Had he not warned her, she would certainly have expected to receive her prop-

erty immediately. Now that she knew that her passport
was at Schabarow it was hard to settle down to anything, but at least she was prepared to wait patiently
two days.

She went to work next day as usual, but she accom-
plished so little that she would have had nothing to eat
had her work card caught the eye of the *Nachalnik*. But
everyone knew that she lived only for the arrival of the
postman, that she could hardly keep her mind on what
she was doing; and the whole camp seemed to be waiting breathlessly with her and was ready to share of its
meals with her.

Thursday dawned, a sunny day with the snow spar-
kling like diamond dust. "Just the day for its arrival,"
she thought as she crunched over the powdery surface
and down to Steputin's office.

"Any mail into today?" she asked. Already her tone
was firmer, her attitude bolder.

"No mail today," he said, hardly looking up and act-
ing just as if he did not know for what she was waiting
so anxiously.

The postman did not come on Friday either. Olga
could not understand the delay.

"But he has always come either Thursday or Friday.
. . . What can be keeping him?" she asked frantically.

She hated to show such anxiety, but the strain was
beginning to tell on her. Her excitement had been so
acute, she had been so buoyed with hope, that the prolonged interval before its fulfilment was more than she
could bear.

Sunday and Monday passed and her old fears began
to torment her again. If her passport had really arrived,

would not the authorities have made some effort to give it to her? After all, the Soviet government owed her something: it was their mistake that she had ever been arrested. So would it not be likely they would make some kind of retribution?

But perhaps the envelope had not been for her after all? This thought sent her quaking back to Bronia again. She found her after work, talking with her brother.

"Look here!" said Anton. "I'm sure it's yours, but I've got to go back to Schabarow tomorrow with another group of prisoners, so I'll put your name on the list and you can come with us. Then you can go to the post office and pick up your passport yourself. It's only five miles from here, and you can manage to find your way back alone."

But she was afraid to do this, afraid that at this late moment she would be punished and lose everything that she had waited for so long. They might arrest her in Schabarow, keep her in the barracks there, take her passport away even. It was all too wildly risky. Had he suggested this at the moment when she had first received the good news, there was nothing she would not have been ready to dare. The mere prospect of getting it filled her with so much courage that she would have defied Steputin himself.

But now that had all seeped away.

"I'm just a cringing creature," she thought; "that's what they do to us here. They break us up; they change our personalities; they make cowards of us, with no will of our own."

"I'll wait," she told Anton; "it's good of you to offer

to take me, but if you're sure it's really mine, maybe it's better to wait till they send it."

She walked back again towards her cabin.

The moon hung full and glittering over the empty scene; round the work shops and sawmill crusted snow cluttered like slag at a pithead. She was tired and cold, and everything seemed utterly hopeless.

Screams shattered the stillness as she passed one of the cabins: sharp blood-curdling cries, mounting in harrowing intensity, but at perfectly regular intervals. It was Moszek, the crazy man. He was like a baby, though he was over fifty. No one knew why he had been brought to camp. He was mad when he was arrested, quietly, decently mad, living harmlessly with his rich old mother. She was with him now, over eighty, but looking after him; he was no trouble, except for his screams that could be heard for blocks. The children teased him, peeping suddenly into his cabin. They did not mean to be cruel, and sometimes brought him pine cones to play with. He would be happy for hours, dropping and picking them up. But they liked to peep at him too, to make him scream.

"You run on home at once," called Olga sharply, coming upon three small boys hiding behind the cook shed. She was sure it was they who had been tormenting Moszek. "And if he screams again," she thought desperately, "I shall go mad too."

The Rabbi's daughter was entering her cabin as Olga went by. She was up now from her attack of pneumonia, emaciated and paler than ever; in the moonlight her eyes burnt black holes in her face, and on her left cheek Olga noticed five livid streaks.

"How's your baby?" she asked, stepping in to visit with the girl, for now that her husband had gone to Schabarow with a poisoned arm, her lot was harder than ever.

"He's better," she answered, struggling to keep her voice steady. "I hope he'll be all right now . . . the peasant's frozen milk doesn't suit him. I've been buying fresh from the teacher, but I don't know whether I'll be able to get any more. . . ."

She began to cry, and suddenly burst out indignantly. "I've been so insulted. . . . I don't know why she did it. . . . I've never been treated like that in my life. . . . I pay her three roubles a pint for her milk. . . . She's let me have it for a week, but when I went today she refused to sell any, and when I begged for just a little, for baby . . . she . . . smacked . . . my face!"

The words came out in a shamefaced rush. To the gentle, shrinking girl such an act was a shocking and incomprehensible brutality.

Olga put her arm around her shoulder and tried to soothe her.

"Let me see your baby," she begged. The girl dried her eyes and lifted the tiny creature from a wooden box where he lay wrapped in a heavy shawl. He was such a puny thing, with his mother's mournful expression already on his little face. But he hardly whimpered when she put him in Olga's arms.

"You keep him so wonderfully," said Olga, marvelling that the girl could wash and press and mend when everything took so much time, and soap and water were so difficult to get.

The cabin too was scrupulously tidy; her father helped her with this. Mrs. Krantz was far too weak to do any housework. She lay on her bed, in the corner, her eyes staring pathetically into the distance.

"Do you think we shall ever get away from here?" she asked suddenly, her thin tired voice breaking the silence.

Olga was moved almost to tears by the hopelessness of their situation, by their patience and uncomplaining courage. "Why, of course we shall," she said, going over to the old lady, putting all the fervour she could summon into her words. "We'll all get away. All of us," she repeated with conviction. "You just get well and everything will come right."

She smiled and gave the baby back to his mother, and walked resolutely through the snow to her own cabin.

"I just don't know how you can stand it!" exclaimed Mrs. Altberg two days later, as the postman still had not shown up in camp.

Olga shrugged her shoulders hopelessly. She felt dispirited and empty, but she had gone back to her old routine, working as seriously as she had done before; getting up to dress and wash in the bitter dark, waiting her turn in line for work and bread. The prisoners no longer asked her about her passport; they knew the postman had not called and guessed what she must be suffering.

Nine leaden days went by and she hid her feelings stoically. It was while she was giving an English lesson to the little Bromberg boy that she reached the end of her tether. It was too dark in the cabin to read or for him to take dictation, so they had conversation, talking slowly of things he knew, of school and sports, of cities and houses, about where he had lived and what he had done; and all at once she was unable to go on. She could no longer sit still, a patient teacher with her little pupil, discussing a life they both had known. She started up, nervously pushing the grammar book from her lap, and as it fell on the floor with a little crash she swayed uncertainly in the darkness, then turned and flung herself on the bench by the table, her head buried in her outstretched arms.

"I can't . . . I can't go on," she sobbed wildly. "I don't know what I shall do, but I can't go on like this!"

Mrs. Bromberg, who had been sitting by the stove, hurried over to her as soon as she realized what had happened. She made a little sign to Tomasz, who tip-toed out of the room and waited with wide-eyed expression in the passage outside. He was very fond of his pretty teacher and this unexpected outburst puzzled and frightened him. Mrs. Bromberg put her hand on Olga's shoulder, but she made no attempt to check the sorrow. "Let her cry," she thought, "it will do her good . . . she's had more than one person can bear." She stood patting her arm and making little sympathetic clucking noises as the frantic weeping continued.

"If it goes on . . ." gulped Olga, "I shall kill myself. . . . I can't live like this. I can't. . . . I want my own life. . . . I want music . . . and beauty . . . and people . . . and friendly cities. I'd rather die than go on here!" and she rolled her head on her arms despairingly.

Mrs. Bromberg put a restraining hand on her hair,

and began stroking it soothingly. "Now, you don't mean that . . . you know you don't. You've been so brave for so long . . . you can be brave a little longer. Why, what would ever happen if your son were to come back and look for you . . . and not be able to find you. . . ."

She stroked and petted and slowly the sobbing ceased. Olga lifted her head from the table, and caught Mrs. Bromberg's hand. "Forgive me," she said. "I didn't mean to give way like that . . . it was just that I felt so desperate and so lonely . . . so . . . ."

"Why, of course," said the other woman encouragingly, "we have all been wondering how you could put up with this long delay. But I'm sure you won't have to wait much longer."

She kissed her and turned away and began busying herself at the stove, stirring the fire and lighting a pine knot, while Olga dried her cheeks and pushed her hair back from her forehead. Mrs. Bromberg took some bread off a shelf and cut three generous slices and put them down to toast.

"Now we'll all have something to eat and you'll feel much better." She called Tomasz and he came into the room, smiling shyly at Olga.

"Watch this bread, dear, and see that it doesn't burn." She began rummaging under her bed and drew out her suitcase. "I've got a little treat for you," she said gaily, as she unlocked the bag and from its depths took out one of Kazia's little cardboard boxes. "This is one of my most precious possessions," she said with an air of great mystery, enjoying the effect she was producing on her two listeners.

They watched her with the greatest expectation until

she pronounced the bread done to a turn. Then Mrs. Bromberg opened the cardboard box, and with reverent fingers, lifted out a large clove of garlic. She rubbed each slice with it very carefully and then put it back into its case. The hot bread now sent up a most appetizing odour, and they all fell to eating with the greatest avidity.

"Mmmmm," said Tomasz between bites, "that's good, Mummy." He rubbed a hand expressively on his little shrunken stomach. "That is exceedingly okay," he added in English, rolling his eyes in comic delight, trying to make Olga laugh.

Orders came that the prisoners could wait inside the store while their work cards were checked, and next day they hastened to get out of the keen air during this interminable chore. It was almost as cold inside the building as out; ice covered the windows and the floor near the door, for the stove had not been lighted, and it was a grey day. As they stood there they heard from the direction of the river the ring of sleigh bells. There was a crack of a whip and the clip-clop of horses' hoofs on the hard ice.

"That's the postman," said a guard . . . and some of the prisoners ran out to watch him; the river had been frozen over for some time but this was the first time they had ever seen it used as a highway. The postman jumped out, throwing his reins over the horse's head; great clouds of steam rose from the animal's shaggy coat but he stood quite quietly at the river edge, although he was not hitched. The postman scrambled up the steep, slippery bank, dragging his canvas bag behind him. He was a cheery, talkative fellow with the great forked beard of a Siberian peasant. He went into the store to wait till Steputin was ready, called out boisterously to the new waitress, and shouted to Icek, who was supposed to look after the stove.

"Thought the ice would never get hard enough to bear me," he exclaimed. "That's the worst of these early winters . . . they're too mild." Olga watched him take the bag into Steputin's office and after some time—long enough, she hoped, for him to have sorted out the letters—she went to him to ask him to give her the passport.

"There is no letter for you," said Steputin as soon as she entered his office.

"Not a letter," she explained doggedly, as if talking to a child who understands with difficulty, "there is a registered envelope for me."

She waited, while he continued to look at her coldly.

"There is nothing for you, I repeat," he said again.

"But I have been told, by someone who saw it, that there is a registered envelope with American seals on it," she insisted angrily. "Look among the registered letters."

He looked into another drawer of the table and shut it again.

"There is a registered letter from the American Embassy in Moscow," he said with a tone of great finality. "But it is not addressed to you."

She could not believe her ears.

Then Anton had been mistaken all along.

Her passport wasn't there. She had had this agonizing expectation, and it had been a false alarm!

She continued to stare at him with unbelieving eyes, and he stared back at her.

"Well, are you satisfied?" His cruel eyes, sprouting from their sockets under bushy enormous eyebrows, dropped beneath her glare. "If you don't believe what I say, you can see for yourself," he added, opening the drawer again and taking out the mail. With maddening deliberation, he went through the lot and held out a large parchment envelope towards her. She almost snatched it from his hand and looked at the name.

"But this *is* mine," she shouted; "look at the address . . . Olga Kochanska. . . . *Can't you read?*" Her voice rose to a shriek.

He did not turn a hair.

"Ah," he said, picking up a pen with an air of complete indifference. "Ah."

She could have struck him in her fury. Had he really made a mistake? Was he playing a trick on her, or was this part of the devilish, soul-torturing system that, without touching so much as a prisoner's hair, could inflict pain beyond human endurance?

She ripped open the envelope, and saw the red passport inside, and as she did so all her anger subsided.

"What does it matter?" she thought. "I'm going to leave all this," she said to herself. "But you have to stay here."

She showed him the passport, contemptuously saying no word, then walked out of the room.

When she had gone a few steps, she turned, re-entered the room, then left it again, banging the door behind her as hard as she could.

9. RELEASE

THAT banged door was the signal of a new life. Release did not come immediately, but camp existence was no longer the same for Olga. She no longer felt abandoned, a woman without a passport, without the backing of an American diplomat who could protest her ill-treatment. To say that she was relieved and happy does not express even a tithe of what she felt at that moment. Only those who have experienced being without a country in a world of ruthless powers can understand to what despair this "statelessness" reduces one, and how any petty tyrant's lust for dominion can take advantage of such a situation. It is the plight of many an unfortunate woman, owing to legislation which, in complicated international issues, has not defined her nationality. And Olga found that without national status there is no legal appeal; there can be no ultimate accounting, for who can champion one's rights when the first of all rights, the recognition of one's very identity, has been denied?

The camp authorities and their subordinates realized

this just as clearly as did Olga, though they did not relinquish their rigid control without a fight.

"Only those who work shall eat," was their rule. But Olga no longer lined up each morning before the *Nachalnik;* except for her share in the odd jobs in the cabin, she refused to work.

She was lucky that the passport came when it did, for she had fallen on an icy path and torn a ligament in her right arm; ordinarily this would not have saved her from the labour gang. When she appeared in the breadline for her daily ration of soup, however, the overseer demanded her work card before allowing her to be served.

"I have no card. I am not working," she told him. It was a new overseer, the third the camp had seen; a handsome, dashing young fellow with a friendly aspect, but much more severe than his predecessors, whose slipshod methods had led to their dismissal—dismissal or worse? The prisoners were never sure that those who watched over them were not prisoners themselves too, or at least being disciplined for political misdemeanours by having to serve a period in comparative exile. They could vent their spleen, and prove their zeal, by unrelenting severity toward their charges, so it seemed; and the new overseer, despite the promise of his charm, evidently was bent on winning a quick discharge, no matter who suffered.

"No work, no food!" he snapped. "Next!" And the breadline moved slowly up, pushing her out of the way.

Olga bounced down to Steputin's office.

She was a different person from the woman who for five months had trembled and pleaded. She demanded her rights; she brandished her passport; she quoted the letter her Consular representative had written telling her to wire him if she were in difficulties. Mr. Ward was responsible for her, she declared, and Steputin must see that she got adequate and sufficient food.

The Commandant listened to her tirade with his customary blank expression, drumming on the table with a huge fist of pinkish well-kept flesh.

"And what are you doing in camp if you are not working?" he demanded coldly.

"I'm waiting to go to the United States!" she shouted; and again she left him, banging the door behind her.

He gave in. She was fed. She took a primitive satisfaction in her victory in that fight for existence. "What is there left for us here," she thought, "but to keep alive . . . that's all."

Now, with the end in sight, she would not let herself be daunted by thoughts of what they might do to her; she was determined not to be starved, or prevented by any other method from leaving the camp.

Keep alive . . . get back to civilization . . . find Johnny. . . . That was her plan. Nor had she any intention of letting them silence her. "For how many will get out alive to tell the tale?" she thought.

Somewhere, behind the scenes, she felt sure, her country was working on her behalf, but a week went by before she had proof of the fact. Henryk came back from the store one morning to tell her that a District Commander was visiting the camp.

"As far as I could understand, he wants to see you," said the boy. "I'd go out and try to contact him. If you don't move, the camp authorities won't lift a hand to help you."

Olga hastily threw on her coat and walked towards the clubhouse. She saw a tall dark man in a handsome Persian lamb coat coming along. When she noted the five-pointed red star with gold lettering in a disc on his lapel, she was sure this was the officer Henryk had spoken of.

"Excuse me," she said in her halting Russian, "are you the *Rei*-Commander?"

"Yes," he answered. "Are you Kochanska?" His manner was pleasant, suave, very different from anything she had encountered in the camp officials.

He invited her to follow him to the Commandant's office for an "investigation."

"May I bring an interpreter?" she asked. She had always spoken Russian without much difficulty, but she wished to have a witness with her now, for she was still not quite sure that, under the pretext of "language difficulties," she might not be forced into unintentional admissions; or that for the same reason a hitch might not occur in the release proceedings.

Her request, however, was readily granted, and she took Anton Minsk along with her.

"You were born in Lemberg," began the Commander.

"No, in Chicago," she said very firmly, feeling that this might play an important part in the investigation. He put a number of questions concerning her life. "And your occupation?"

"I am a violinist," she answered.

"A violinist!" he exclaimed enthusiastically, interest lighting his fine eyes. He did not pursue the subject, though he seemed to be considering her very carefully. He asked many questions concerning her arrest, and the time she had spent in camp, writing at length in an official-looking document.

"Let me see," he said, reading it over as if not sure that he had all the information he required. "You were born in Warsaw, were you not?"

"No, I said Chicago," she insisted. "And I mean Chicago!"

He left, apparently satisfied with the interview, and a day or two later the prisoners noted a little wooden cart, with heavy wooden wheels, standing outside the general store. The overseer from Gary had driven over, his sturdy little horse clipping off the twenty miles in good time in spite of the snow and frost. Now the poor animal was standing perfectly still, no rug covering him after his exertions, and with nothing to keep him from moving around, though the district overseer had gone inside for a meal and would probably spend the rest of the day at the camp. The prisoners, waiting their turn for soup, sniffed appreciatively the smell of hot fat in which his *pelmenis*—that national dish of chopped meat in little dough balls—had been fried. A bluish smoke rose from the kettle of boiling grease; "like incense," thought the famished Poles, who had tasted no fats for five months.

Olga went over to the overseer to tell him that Mr. Ward had wired her to "report to Moscow immediately."

"But how am I to get away from here?" she asked anxiously. "How do I go about to get released? No one here suggests doing anything. And how can I possibly travel without warm clothes to wear?"

The overseer was most helpful and explicit.

"You must make a formal application to the N.K.W.D. in Moscow, requesting your release, and add a petition for money and adequate clothes for the journey," he said.

"Will it take long?" asked Olga, somewhat appalled at the thought of making a "formal" application.

"About six weeks, I should think," answered the overseer.

"My God!" exclaimed Olga. "As long as that!"

She wondered what form of address a petition to the dreaded secret police should take, and foresaw endless delays owing to possible incorrect procedure. She twisted uncertainly on her bench before the overseer.

"Would you tell me just what to write?" she pleaded. "Or maybe . . . you would write it yourself?"

He wrote the letter for her and promised to post it in Gary. She had not liked to suggest that letters posted in camp never seemed to reach their destination, so her relief was great when he offered to take hers with him.

Once more she faced another long period of waiting, though this time her suffering was not so great for she was not afraid. The panicky feeling that had overwhelmed her sometimes before had gone, and she knew that all she had to do was to endure the daily tedium and discomfort, just stick it through. But how the time dragged!

Now that she could ignore the shouted orders, and the guards' incessant coercion no longer stifled her reason, she tried to review her imprisonment objectively and to understand the implacable gaoler who commanded the camp. She had been like a draught animal before, performing her tasks blindly, but as she looked back on the desolate, hungry days, the aimless work, the needless waiting in queues at all hours, she wondered what Steputin hoped to accomplish by reducing the exiles to a level of shiftless squalor.

"He tries to crush our spirits, he punishes us for conditions imposed by himself and which not one of us has even encountered before; but what is his plan? What is he doing with us here? Does he know himself?"

It was hard to answer. She realized that it might have been very much worse. Lemberg citizens exiled to Kazakstan would no doubt envy the life at Zimny Gorodok. What luck she had had in narrowly escaping exile to any other penal colony. More and more prisoners were leaving each day for Lejkin. "Black Beauty" had gone; Bronia Minsk had gone; one woman, a first-class nurse, had been condemned to a special sentence of hard labour in the barracks there. She had been implicated in the escape of five prisoners, although the evidence against her seemed singularly inconclusive.

It was the first time that anyone had attempted to break loose. There was no stockade round the camp; the prisoners were not locked up at night; there were not even locks on their doors. Steputin relied as much upon the inaccessibility of the district for their safe confinement as upon the scores of armed guards continually on the lookout.

But these men had got away. Why was the woman

accused? She had bought the teakettle of one of the fugitives a short time previously.

"And she must have known that he intended to escape, else why would he have parted with such a valuable possession?" argued Steputin.

It was a type of reasoning the Poles found particularly baffling. But Steputin's severity was always illogical.

Mr. Fischer and Mr. Hind found their names on the list of those ordered to Lejkin. Both were terribly concerned about leaving their wives alone, and to Josef Fischer the prospect of the strenuous barrack life was particularly disturbing as he was sure his heart could not stand the strain.

When the time came for the convoy to start out, Mr. Fischer and Mr. Hind were missing.

The guard on duty searched the cabins, hunted through the camp, called their names, and when they still failed to turn up, fetched the Commandant. Steputin made a terrible to-do, shouting and threatening, firing his revolver into the air. But the two men, quaking under the potatoes in the cook-shed cellar, did not come out; and after a long time the commotion subsided, the guard left with his other prisoners, and nothing more was said about the matter.

Was Steputin relaxing his vigilance? Growing soft? Olga found that hard to believe. He probably had deep-laid plans. He had surprised Olga recently by speaking to her of the possibility of organizing music in camp. But she immediately suspected his motives.

"There may be other musicinas among the prisoners,"

he observed. "You might form an orchestra and conduct it yourself!"

Was he trying to placate her now that he knew she was leaving? Olga could not make out if he were ironical or in earnest or just raising hopes for the pleasure of thwarting them. The last seemed probably true.

She had known him to reward prisoners for good behaviour by promising to send them to a penal colony near some big town. Yet everyone who had worked in such places reported that the life was much harder there, and the food even worse than at Zimny Gorodok.

His was a twisted, pitiless nature; he overlooked no opportunity to increase the suffering of those within his power. Even if he were really undergoing imprisonment in camp himself, as the prisoners sometimes suspected, the extent to which he exceeded his authority could hardly be explained by the simple urge for revenge. He devised such subtle means to wound the human spirit, it seemed as if the man derived a secret delight from the infliction and sight of pain.

Only a short time before, a new group of prisoners had arrived in camp from a penal colony in another district. They were shifted because work there was exhausted and the Commandant was dispersing them until spring. Among them was a gaunt, bent woman, her eyes dimmed and sunken as though from constant weeping. Once she must have been beautiful, with a lively expression on her sensitive features; now she stared straight before her, as if always seeking something, and hardly seemed to heed the people about her. She had been two days in camp, assigned to one of the furthermost cabins, and had not appeared yet in the breadline, though no one knew how she ate. The first day she went to work, she was set to hauling wood and later took her place in line, clutching at a heavy shawl around her head and shoulders, when the other prisoners heard a sudden scream as one of them took his plate of soup over to a cook-shed table.

"Edmond! Edmond!" cried the woman.

The man turned as if he had been shot, put down his soup, and rushed over to the newcomer. "Anna!" he shouted. "Is it really you?"

He put his arms around her, dragging her from the long queue, smothering her with kisses.

"It's my wife," he explained to the astonished prisoners. "She missed our train. She was left behind. . . ."

He could hardly speak for emotion, and the woman was almost fainting.

They retired to a corner of the shed, talking, crying, laughing a little, telling each other of their experiences. It seemed a miracle that they should have met again this way. The husband had been like a madman when, at one of the stations during their journey from Lemberg, she had wandered away to get milk for her baby and the train had gone on without her. He had made agonizing efforts to persuade the guard, first to let him off to find her, and then to telegraph to her. Neither entreaties nor bribes brought any results. Even at Zimny Gorodok Steputin declared he was unable to trace the woman, although, he callously asserted, she could not possibly be lost, but "merely mislaid, probably at another camp."

Now they were together again, incredulous at their own joy, gazing at each other as though fearing the meeting was a dream. One of the woman's first questions was about their child, but her words came slowly and with difficulty. She was loathe to risk turning this meeting to sorrow and she dreaded to hear the answer. How could a tiny thing survive conditions such as she had known? Her broken body told its own tale; but her heart was so hungry for news that she was ready to sacrifice those first wonderful moments to ask about her baby.

Prisoners who had been watching the reunion felt a proprietary glow in the happiness of the two, and when the woman asked about her child they all wanted to shout out that the baby boy was well, that they had helped take care of him at first, and that now he was in the newly opened Soviet nursery. It was so rare that they shared good news, or that there was ever an occasion to rejoice; but how their hearts leapt up when the opportunity occurred.

In the same way they felt as stricken as did the parents when Steputin refused to let them claim the child. The mother would look at her baby so wistfully in the few moments when she was allowed to visit him in the nursery; it was such bitter grief being forbidden to take care of him herself after the long separation. But the Commandant had no intention of permitting the young couple to extract this satisfaction from the odd chance that brought them together again; he saw to it that they did not work together; nor did he allow her to move from the cabin at the end of the row where she had originally been assigned. But here the prisoners took matters into their own hands, and one of the husband's cabin mates moved out and took the woman's hut, so that at least the two could spend their leisure time together. And if any of the guards noted the change they said nothing.

An innovation and an improvement in the camp was the opening of the bathhouse. The prisoners themselves had built this under the direction of an overseer from another colony, and they had every reason to feel proud of their efforts, considering their own inexperience and the conditions under which they had to work. It was a big cabin of the type they all lived in—rough adze-hewn logs piled one on another, their ends interlacing at the four corners, the space between them packed with clay and heavy moss. A small window at each side admitted a little light. No Siberian window is ever made to open, but air was not lacking from around the lop-sided window frames.

The native Siberian can fashion almost anything with an axe and a brace; village houses are made with no other tools; planks and joints are held in place with wooden pegs only. Under the czars, iron nails were worth more than their weight in gold, and Olga, who had spent many a long day hammering straight the few rusty ones available, came to the conclusion that under Soviet rule they were equally precious. But, lacking Siberian deftness in handling an axe and hammering pegs, the Poles found construction of this kind particularly difficult and the building proceeded very slowly.

Finally, however, the camp was allowed to inspect the result. The cabin stood solidly, twenty feet square, its plank floor a step above the ground, the slats of its pointed roof held in place by longitudinal strips of wood nailed at each end. A wall of double planks wedged tight with sawdust cut the cabin in two, and one half was divided by a light partition into two cubicles each containing two shelves or platforms, one above the other, like berths in a railway compartment, capable of accommodating about a dozen persons each.

Bricks covered the back wall of these cubicles, in the midst of which was a stove, a kind of temple reaching from floor to ceiling. When the stove had been well heated, a pail of water was thrown against the hot bricks, filling the cubicles with steam, in which the bathers, on their shelves, were supposed to stew.

The prisoners were told they could use the bathhouse at a charge of seventy kopeks per person, but at first they were slow to take advantage of the offer. The price was the equivalent of a day's work, a big sum to pay for the dubious pleasure of this Russian form of bathing to which the Poles were not accustomed. Nor did they find very attractive the prospect of cooling off in the draughty cabin with a bucket of cold water to wash off the violent effect of the steaming. Russians are a hardy people and this strenuous form of bathing was borrowed from the tough Finnish peasants. Scratch a Siberian and you find a Finn; for the former, too, loves to emerge from the steamy heat and throw himself, naked, into the snow outside, the better to relish the shock of sharply contrasted sensations. Bathing for him is an occasion for social intercourse; it takes several hours, and is associated with eating and drinking and gratifications of a similar nature.

This leisurely, pleasurable atmosphere was naturally lacking for the Poles, who had no time to spare and were concerned merely in getting clean. Three of the younger prisoners persuaded Olga to join them one day when the intense cold made work for them all impossible, but she was very diffident at first about doing so. The idea of communal bathing shocked her, and she was afraid that the violent changes of heat and cold would bring on neuralgia. But the girls were friendly and insistent, and she was feeling low and despondent over the long delay in her release, so she decided to accompany them. They were students from Posen University—the baby-faced Hania and her sister Sozia, and another girl but recently invalided home from Lejkin.

The bath attendant was cleaning the place when they entered, swabbing down water which ran out of holes at one end of the cabin. He was a fair, elegant-looking man, a wealthy Pole who had once been one of Dr. Altberg's patients: "Bobi," his friends called him; even in camp he was jolly and full of high spirits. He wore a grey-blue sweater and shorts while he worked, and was one of the few who had known and enjoyed luxurious steam baths before, so he tried to create the appropriate atmosphere for his clients.

"Ah, *pani* Kochanska! I'm delighted to see you," he exclaimed as the women entered. "I'll have the tea ready immediately!"

The girls giggled at the professional manner he put on—as if there were really tea! "You'll be taking massage afterwards?" he inquired with mock solicitude. "What . . . no massage? Too bad, too bad. I'm feeling very strong today."

The girls laughed more than ever—nobody but Bobi made little jokes with them—and went over to the side where a woman attendant was waiting. They stripped, leaving their clothes hanging in the front part of the cabin, and entered a cubicle which was full of steam.

The temperature, as they stood on the floor, was not very hot, but when they mounted the steps to the first shelf, the steam was distinctly fiercer, while up on the second it was almost more than they could bear. The moist, close atmosphere reduced them to quiescent languor; they could feel the sweat start trickling down their thighs and backs. They were lying on the shelf gasping, the cloud of steam almost blinding them, when Hania gave a little squeal. From her perch she could just see through a bit of the tiny windowpane.

"There's *'Ponuri'!*" she called. "He's coming this way, and he's with his bride." The others crowded to catch a glimpse of Steputin's wife, who had but recently arrived in camp.

The prisoners had all been personally interested when they heard she was coming and had cherished great hopes concerning the possible effects of her softening influence; but they had been speedily disillusioned by her sullen face and cold, unfriendly manner.

"Either she hates the camp, or she hates Steputin," they reasoned, watching the awkward, big-framed girl striding moodily in their midst, shabbily dressed; unkempt bobbed fair hair pushed back from her untamed eyes.

But the two seemed less morose as they strolled over to the bathhouse. Could this indeed be their *"Ponuri,"* their "sourpuss," whose only joy was denying someone a right, this man who was talking animatedly to his companion, who called out almost boisterously to Bobi and told him to get busy?

"But he can't come in today; it's women's day!" whispered little Hania in shocked tones.

Yet it was quite evident that the Commandant not only had every intention of coming in but of taking a bath as well.

They could hear him moving about the cabin outside, still talking to his bride; and soon the door of the other cubicle opened and slammed again. There were whispered exclamations and laughing as the two climbed to an upper shelf.

Olga and her companions sat stiff with embarrassment. Had Bobi told the Commandant that the second cubicle was occupied?

"It probably wouldn't have made any difference to *them*," sneered Sozia, with the condemnation of the very young.

Certainly the couple next door seemed oblivious of everything but themselves, chatting, giggling, moving noisily on the wooden platform.

"Bobi, more water!" shouted Steputin; and the attendant slipped back the circular opening pierced in the heavy partition and deftly tossed through it a bucket of water. This action required a great deal of skill, for the sudden escape of steam could have burnt his hands. The couple inside must have been adepts, too, adjusting their positions to the sudden increase of steam and heat. There was a jumping and bumping; their cries and exclamations grew louder as the atmosphere became thicker.

"Now the birches!" called out Steputin, and Bobi

handed two large bundles of twigs through the opening.

Hania gasped. "What are they going to do?" she asked in a frightened whisper.

"You flick yourself to work up the circulation," answered Olga, remembering her life in Kiev. "It's the customary thing in a Russian bath; everyone does it."

The thin little whistle of whips on flesh came distinctly from the other side of the partition; it pattered and faltered and rose again, quicker and louder, so that the listeners shuddered as though the red weals marked their own quivering flanks.

"More . . . more!" Steputin's voice was thick and blurred; they could hear him rolling heavily on the wooden shelf.

"Come . . . come . . . more . . . let me show you." There was a scuffle, and more lashing and little cries. "No . . . no . . . you're hurting. . . ." It was the woman's voice that rang out suddenly; but it was quickly drowned in the heavy breathing and grunting of the other. The volume of steam rose and the whipping increased in violence; the two were working each other into a wild exultation, saturated in the heavy vapour, covered with sweat and excited by the dark striping that laddered their bare bodies.

"How can they keep it up?" whispered Hania, her eyes starting with horror, as the whips rose and fell in rhythmical savagery.

"Don't listen to them," urged Olga, sick with disgust, and wishing she had never come with the girls. Burning clouds of steam blinded them and they seemed to be stewing in a veritable hell as the sounds next door redoubled their urgency. Heavy bodies pounded the slippery platform, the slap of wet buttocks punctuated the whistling of the birches. Like two animals, snarling and wrestling, they panted with the intoxication of their exertions; Steputin's voice was no longer human as his long-drawn-out "uhhr . . . uhhr . . . uhhrs . . ." came hoarsely through the thudding and flogging.

"Do you think we should go now?" asked Sozia a long time afterwards, when silence had fallen on the pair next door.

"No . . . let them get out first. I don't want to see them," screamed Olga, her nerves on edge.

She could hardly breathe in the thick atmosphere, but they all waited till the other two slipped from their bench and came out of the cubicle. They could hear Steputin calling curtly for cold water, in tones the prison knew so well, then sounds of splashing and rinsing as they sent great jets spouting over themselves. When they had gone, the four women staggered out and gingerly dipped up some hot water from a big cauldron to mix with the bucket of cold which the woman attendant brought them.

Icy air from outside blew through the cracks round the window; the puddles on the floor were already freezing over. More women had entered the bathhouse; one of them was washing her hair in a pail used for rinsing. Olga wrinkled her nose in disgust as she hurried into her clothes. They left the place in silence, weak and limp from the experience.

"All the same," insisted Hania, as they parted to go to their own cabins, "Steputin shouldn't have come on women's day. He must know quite well that on Saturday the bathhouse is reserved for us."

Olga made no answer. Steputin's attitude was clear to her now.

Saturdays . . . Sundays . . . Mondays . . . the days crawled by for Olga, bringing no change. Her patience was beginning to ebb again; once more her thoughts took the form of "*if* I ever get out" instead of of the "*when* I get out" in which she had been indulging; it was so long since she had sent her petition to Moscow she feared she was again forgotten. Christmas was in sight, and the glistening fir trees in the forest seemed a daily mockery, with their reminder of the festive season and all that it meant in a free land.

Each morning along the river's edge their green-black twigs were delicately outlined in hoar-frost, but the surface of the great ice highway, where peasants drove their sleds and horses, was gradually becoming drab and grey with the dust which slowly accumulated on it. Would she ever leave along this smooth hard road, she wondered.

During her free hours she often walked down to scan its immense length as it curved like an iron rail disappearing in the black emptiness. From all around her came the sound of axes and falling trees. The men were working in the forests, cutting and hauling; and most of the women were stacking the logs in neat square piles, plunging in and out of the snowy underbrush to collect their heavy loads.

They had been told that work would go on as usual at the "Christmas-tree holiday," which was how Soviet authorities referred to December twenty-fifth! This severity was possibly due to the increased restrictions imposed after the escape; but the prisoners hoped against hope that at least there would be something extra to eat; not holiday fare, nothing good, of course, but just a double portion of bread, perhaps; an additional spoonful of barley in their soup. They had learned to moderate their desires and curb their appetites, but it was difficult to forget what day this was.

Christmas Eve was a sad anniversary for them all; even the guards about the camp were unhappy and surly: penalties the prisoners paid increased their duties too. The older men among them surely remembered with what veneration this day had always been observed in olden times; while the day following had been an even greater festival.

Christmas used to be theirs by right; there was not another holiday like it in all the year. Not even a convict could be made to work that day; and the poorest peasant put aside his labours and rejoiced in the midst of his family.

There were those who had memories, too, of the rich food they had had when they ran their own Siberian co-operatives on their individual holdings; the sucking pigs, geese and fat ducks they had eaten; the partridges, hazel hen, and quail that were theirs for the hunting; plentiful salmon hanging thick in long brown fringes to dry under the fretted eaves of their porches; great fragrant loaves of white bread sprinkled with poppy seed; such tubs of golden butter they used it to grease the axles of their cartwheels; tasty cheeses and heaped-up round stones of frozen curd.

Even when Russia starved, western Siberia had been a land of plenty and clung to its traditions and customs long after Communist levelling elsewhere. Slowly the skeleton hand of penury caught up with them, as economic conditions were sacrificed to political ends.

Thoughts like these soured the faces of the sentinels; but what the prisoners felt most at the suppression of this feast day was a sensation of total isolation, for to work at Christmas was to lose communion with the rest of Europe.

The Hinds had asked Olga to spend the evening with them, and after the day's work was over she walked down to their cabin. Mrs. Hind had curled her hair and had on a pretty silk dress; her husband wore a new dark suit. It was like a real party. They had cut branches of pine to put in their window, and standing in the middle of the room in an iron pot was a little Christmas tree. No gifts decorated its branches, but at the top burned a little light—a vigil for the Christ Child. Mrs. Hind had hollowed out half a potato, and in the oil with which she had filled it floated a twist of flaming thread.

They talked over old times together, of the parties they used to give in Warsaw at Christmas time, of dropping in to the Europeski for coffee and cakes, and supper after the theatre at Simon and Stecki. Olga thought wistfully of midnight Mass with Waclaw at the Cathedral . . . and then they sang carols, and did their best to be happy, and if one saw another's eyes filling with tears, he or she strove valiantly to banish the thoughts and memories that crowded in at the sight.

"Christ is born. 'Good will on earth; peace among men,'" they sang defiantly, they sang courageously.

There had been no extra rations, not even a slice of bread; but Mrs. Hind produced a small can of corned beef for the Christmas dinner, a remnant of the provisions she had brought on the long journey from Lemberg, and which, for some strange reason, she had never wanted to open; so they really had a celebration and told each other that next Christmas would see them all at home!

When Olga rose to leave, snow was falling heavily. Mr. Hind wanted to accompany her to her cabin, but she would not hear of it. "That's no way to end a cozy evening," she declared, unwilling to drag him into the storm, and she set out to walk the distance alone. Only two blocks north and six to the east; she had to pass the sawmill and canteen, but even in the swirling darkness she felt sure she could find her way home.

A fearful roaring shook the forest; she had never known such a night. Was this one of the *burans*, the late winter blizzards that suddenly sweep over Siberia?

She hugged her coat about her, lowered her head to the wind and pushed on. The night was completely dark, and the snow plastered her eyelids, stinging her eyes. She could not catch her breath in the icy cold; it cut the very life from her as she staggered and clutched at the side of one of the cabins.

"Shall I go back?" she thought, afraid of the black space before her in which she could see no outline. She plunged forward again, but fell into a snowdrift waist deep; the path seemed bewitched; she had gone this way a hundred times, and now she was lost and unable to get her bearings. She picked herself up, trying vainly to brush the snow from her clothes, but the whirling flakes blinded her and seemed jeering at her efforts.

She groped for a cabin again and cautiously followed its wall, but when she reached the end and started for the next, the distance between them perplexed and appalled her. She must be walking diagonally . . . she had got into the next lane . . . how could she find her way back to her own cabin . . . at this rate?

A great weariness overcame her; the wind pierced steel razors through her body; again she felt a baffling white mass before her; she did not know which way to turn and was so tired she did not greatly care. Suddenly, to lie down and die seemed an infinitely simple solution.

The snow was so white . . . so soft on the ground . . . she would have such a little while to wait . . . no one could last long in that temperature . . . all her troubles would be so quickly over. She stumbled forward and sank on her knees . . . it was so easy . . . so restful.

"But Jan . . . what about Jan?" rang like a bell in her consciousness. Horrified at her own action, she pulled herself together.

"I must be going crazy," she thought. "A little snow and wind . . . what of it!" Setting her teeth, she walked twenty steps resolutely and felt the shutters on the canteen windows. "Now straight on . . . twenty more." She paced the way, counting and gasping . . . the third cabin . . . the fourth. . . . She reached her home and grasped the latch which Mr. Fischer had made for their door. It took her some time to open it, and she fell into the room.

"A merry Christmas!" muttered Dr. Altberg, waking up and turning in his bed. She lay panting, her hand at her side, bent almost double. "A merry Christmas," she whispered.

She did not count the days after that: they came and went in bleak procession. She hardly left the cabin except to eat and was worn and weak with waiting and despair. One night, as she dozed in the icy room, she was aroused by a tremendous pounding on the door.

In the darkness the sudden noise was terrifying: the camp echoed with the shattering blows. She started from her bed, and crept barefooted to the passage outside the room, afraid that someone would break in. "Who is there?" she called in a trembling voice.

Steputin answered, stern and chill, from the blackness of the night:

"Get ready at once. Pack your things. You are to go to Moscow."

10. THE JOURNEY BACK

Olga stood stock still listening to Steputin's voice on the other side of the cabin door. Then she put on her coat and unfastened the latch with fingers that quaked with fear and excitement. He was waiting in the snow outside, an iron candlestick in his hand, in which a bit of candle burned, shielded by a thick glass chimney.

"Get ready," he repeated in a tone of annoyance, "don't stand there shivering. You've no time to lose."

She was bewildered by his sudden appearance, by the unconventional hour at which she had been aroused with orders to depart, after having waited over six weeks without sign or word from those responsible for her imprisonment.

"Am I to go now, in the middle of the night?" she asked blankly. "How can I travel in this weather?"

"It's already morning," he said, "it's nearly four o'clock." He added, "And as for your travelling, you're to have *my* fur coat . . . if you wish to know." This in very surly accents, for it was evident that this order rankled.

Olga could not help smiling a little maliciously. To depart in the Commandant's own coat was an exit she had not dreamed of even in her wildest flights of fancy; and she felt that some higher authority must have had an ironic understanding of infinite psychological profoundities to furnish her with this particular little personal triumph.

"I'll dress and pack at once," she said breathlessly. "You return to your house, and I'll come along when I am ready."

But she had hardly put on her clothes when he was back again at her cabin door, suspicious as ever, unwilling to leave her alone a moment.

"Hurry, hurry," he urged, "a man has driven over from Gary to get you, and the horse will freeze if you don't make haste."

That was the first time she had ever heard Steputin considering the condition of a horse, and she knew this was but a pretext to get her away quickly.

The Altbergs had been awakened by the violent knocking and were up helping her to get ready; the Fischers too were dressed. Henryk had immediately left to waken some of their friends in other cabins to collect from them letters and addresses that Olga might get in touch with their relatives in Poland and abroad. They had not risked giving her these before for they never knew if or when their possessions were searched; and now, with her precipitate departure it looked as if this grace-given opportunity would be lost. Henryk realized the terrible possibility, and the moment Steputin's back was turned darted off on his mission. It would be tragic if such a chance were missed: Olga was their hope, their messenger, their one link with the free world, someone whom they could trust and whose promise would not fail, yet it was obviously Steputin's intention to frustrate any such scheme.

"Aren't you ready yet?" he demanded, fuming and stamping in the cabin. "That suitcase is packed, why don't you come?"

"I am waiting for Henryk," said Olga boldly. "He went to get me some bread."

"What do you want bread for?" shouted Steputin, exasperated.

Olga felt she was on safe ground now. He dared not refuse her food, she knew that; and the delay, with the canteen probably closed at this hour, would seem perfectly natural.

"I am not going without food," she said obstinately. "I don't know how long this journey will take, but I am sure my diplomatic representative would not like to hear that I left the camp without any provisions, not even a crust of dry bread."

Her argument was unanswerable. Steputin could rage as much as he liked, but under the circumstances he could not force her to leave.

She stood in the cabin with her friends about her. Now that the actual moment of her departure had come she felt that leaving them was a desertion. She put her arms around them, almost hating to go. They crowded about her, clasping her hands, rejoicing for her sake, sorrowful for their own, and still not completely convinced that she was really on her way to her own country and would reach there safely.

Kazia and the Imp sobbed aloud like little girls.

Olga's good-humoured courage made a big difference to their lives. She had been so much with them the last six weeks, working around the cabin, they knew they would miss her terribly. Mrs. Altberg and Mrs. Fischer were crying too. From the first days of the nightmare railway journey they had been attracted to this gracious, gallant figure, and under all the strain of their cramped quarters there had never been a wry word between them. Always she had been tactful and accommodating. As for the men, they made no attempt to hide their despair at seeing her go. Tears rolled down their cheeks unheeded. It was not merely the loss of a good companion, a woman who, even under the shocking changes wrought by harsh living and allowing for their own frozen desires, unconsciously challenged their manhood; there was about her some glowing eagerness, a quality of exaltation which stripped their minds of non-essentials, and a hunger for beauty and for music that quickened their perception of abiding values. Somehow she had sustained and stimulated them; yet her timidity, and something childlike in her manner, roused their protective instincts. They felt responsible for her; even now as she said good-bye, they were anxious for her safety. And at Steputin's rising impatience and repeated orders, she became uneasy too.

"It is so strange your going off like this in the dark," muttered Dr. Altberg, "with no warning or time for preparation."

Olga's eyes were brilliant with excitement and apprehension.

"If you don't hear from me soon," she whispered,

"will you inform my consul what happened? You know the address?"

Mrs. Altberg nodded, and the doctor put a finger on his lips, for Steputin was at the door again.

"Here's the coat," he said curtly, pushing into the room without warning.

Olga took the heavy thing in her arms, and they helped her into it. It was rough fur outside, bear or wolf; in the dim light she could not tell. The lining was thick lamb's wool, warm and comforting. It hung almost to the ground, enveloping her slight body in its generous folds. The collar rose high about her cheeks, touching the knitted cap she had pulled over her ears. Only her feet were unprotected; her overshoes had long since worn to shreds and all she had on were a pair of light walking shoes over silk stockings. She lifted one foot into the warmth of the overcoat. Mrs. Altberg noted the gesture.

"Take these," she said generously, reaching beside her bunk and picking up the boots she had bought at the store. They were her *czunia*, the cloth soles with high quilted leggings that Siberian peasants wear.

"But what will you do without them?" protested Olga.

"Take them," ordered Steputin sternly, and Olga put them on.

"I'll send them back to you," she whispered, and was about to add more when Henryk burst into the room.

"Did you get the bread?" called Olga quickly. "Give it to me."

Henryk, seeing Steputin, needed no warning. He went over to her as she stood with her handbag open, and slipped into her hand a tiny package which she immediately hid under her handkerchief and purse.

"Canteen wasn't open. I had to borrow some. I was afraid I was going to miss you," panted the boy. He looked around at the others and at Steputin's forbidding countenance, then at Olga as they all tearfully surrounded her, realizing this was the last time he might ever see her.

"I don't know what we shall do without you, but it's so wonderful for you," he began, then broke off and threw his arms around her neck and kissed her—not Polish fashion, politely on either cheek, but full on the mouth.

Immediately all the others did the same. They clung to her, straining her in their arms as they wished her Godspeed, kissing her and turning to wipe their tears. Something seemed to die within them as they watched her go. Steputin looked on contemptuously, pulling at the door impatiently.

"You must come at once," he declared; "I can't wait any longer."

She tore herself from the embraces of her friends, these dear ones whom she suddenly found closer to her than anyone she had ever known, and whom perhaps she would never see again. Her heart seemed breaking.

Then she called to Steputin, who was disappearing into the darkness:

"You've forgotten my baggage. Please carry it!" To the astonishment of everyone in the cabin, he came back, picked up her suitcase and roll of rugs and marched off into the night.

Olga waved a final farewell and walked slowly down

the snowy path, her eyes full of tears. The fur coat
hung heavily on her shoulders, almost overwhelming
her, but the comfort of its protection against the steely
cold more than compensated for its weight. She snug-
gled her hands in her little muff and watched with immense satisfaction Steputin ahead of her, walking awkwardly with a heavy load in each hand.

"I dragged those myself when I arrived," she thought
girmly, "now he has to carry them!" A soldier was
standing next to a little wooden sleigh outside the
Commandant's house, swinging his arms and stamping
his feet, trying to get warm. Steputin called to him to
take the baggage, and the man sprang to attention and
put it on the sled, which had no seat. Then he knocked
the snow off his boots and stepped in, standing up in
front as he seized the reins. He cracked his whip and
began clucking and calling to the weary horse.

Without a word, Steputin pointed to the sled, and
Olga got in, sitting on her suitcase, and arranging the
fur coat carefully around her to cover her feet. The
horse seemed to wake up and started to move. Still
Steputin did not speak. He did not even deign to say
good-bye as they drove off, but stood watching the de-
parting figures for a moment, then shrugged his shoulders and turned into his cabin, shutting the door noisily
behind him.

Olga and the soldier drove in silence a long time.
The stick-straight legs of the little horse broke into a
steady trot; in the parching frost every hair of his
shaggy coat was silhouetted in fretted mahogany. They
passed through the long lane between the cabins and
made off in the direction of the forest, where ruts from

the runners on the packed, dry snow showed faintly clear in the dead light of a moon emerging reluctantly from clouds.

Olga blinked as the piercing air seared her eyes and throat. Never had she breathed such cold, and she hugged herself luxuriantly in the massive folds of the coat.

A great joy surged with the warmth through her body as they left the camp behind. Her heart danced; she wanted to cry out and sing; and she found herself making wonderful resolutions for the future. This was the beginning—this ride through the snowy forest—the beginning of her freedom, of a new existence for her. How she would treasure, now, every precious moment of it! Never again would she take the lovely things life offered without immediate recognition of their value. She would be humbly grateful for each small satisfaction, for every crumb of love. "Time is so short," she thought. "I have so much to make amends for. I did not stop to think before how little I responded to affection; I must not keep love hidden; I cannot be so reticent. To my loved ones I must break this seal of silence. I must show my mother how I love her, make her understand how deep my feelings are. They never knew. I never showed them. I took so much for granted. . . . Love is so important. . . .

"And if Jan is still alive, I must make him understand too. . . ."

Thoughts of her home-coming flooded her being; it would be different now; she must make it different.

The moon sailed cold and brilliant in the heavens,

five lesser moons reflected about it; great stars hung so low she felt she could have reached them.

She gazed over the icy landscape, peering at the fantastic tree-shapes, her vision glued on the fairy crystals, a world of enchanting strangeness opened around her; she looked and looked, unable to move her eyes for wonder, and slowly realized that her eyelids were stiff and frozen. The soldier grinned and pointed to a cabin ahead of them. It was the beginning of Schabarow; and soon they were passing the high picket fences that kept the wolves from the wooden dwellings of this sprawling village.

They stopped at a house larger than the others, which belonged, said the soldier, to a Soviet official. He hurried Olga into the living room, where a sleepy woman was trying to light the stove, and a sluttish-looking girl was pushing around the dirt on the floor with a worn-out broom.

Hardly a word was spoken. The occupants of the house showed no surprise at Olga's entrance. Apparently they had been warned of her arrival, though there was nothing for her to eat, and not so much as a drop of hot water to drink. She was glad to come in, however; even the sour stuffiness of the room was a relief after the aching cold outside. She dropped onto a wooden bench and gently massaged her tingling eyes to release the rigid lids. It was a dismal enough place, this official's house, hardly better, though much larger, than the cabin she had lived in at Zimny Gorodok. But she did not stay long; the soldier soon left her, going to the horse's head to rub his nostrils and eyes, which were white with frost, then calling to Olga to resume the trip.

She tucked herself in on her suitcase, and watched the man in his long khaki coat as he clucked and talked to his sturdy little nag. On his head he wore the characteristic felt skull cap of the Russian infantry, a *cicka*, the prisoners at Zimny Gorodok used to call it, which was not a very pretty word, though the cap really was rather like a woman's breast with a funny little nipple on top.

Light was beginning to waver in the sky and the sun came slowly over the edge of the world. Bands of vibrating colour shot like lightning through the forest; the crystals in the trees caught fire and blazed in a jewelled glitter; intricate geometric figures clung to the dark-green branches; whole scenes with animals, houses, and people seemed to build themselves before her, each snowflake brittle and perfect with elaborate, gem-cut edges.

With the huddle of houses behind them, the countryside was empty again; no sign of a living soul in the midst of all this extravagant decoration.

The full glory of a new day poured over the limitless snowy stretches.

The soldier pointed his whip at the flaming sky.

"Look!" he said. "Look! sunrise! Do you have sunrise in America?"

Olga thought of golden light flooding Illinois corn fields—and of stalwart barns and rich farmhouses, with breakfast in the kitchen of hot, sweet coffee, and pans of yellow cream, with buckwheat cakes, sausages and fried eggs and maple syrup. . . .

"Yes," she said dreamily, "we have sunrise in America."

"Fine!" said the soldier. "Great country, America."

Olga agreed that it was a great country.

"But unemployment has assumed dimensions you are unable to cope with, and you treat your Negroes disgracefully . . . there is no equality there," added the man in a little rush.

Olga could not help laughing at the parrot phrase. She had heard it before. All the Russian guards knew about the penniless vagrants of America and what a bad time coloured folks had.

"But they forgot to tell him about the sunrise . . . he didn't know the sun rises too . . ." she mused.

They were coming to a long incline, and the soldier suggested they walk to spare the horse. Olga was glad of an opportunity to stretch her legs; they plodded over hills and across bridges; she felt the journey would never end. Once again they stopped to rest and unfreeze in a village, then on again—the drive was becoming interminable. At one point they saw languid smoke rising from a smouldering forest fire. The little horse's ears twitched nervously and he slackened speed, snuffing suspiciously. Their trail crossed a burnt-out gash, where charred birches swayed precariously, and lurking flames still flickered round the resinous stumps of pines. By twelve they were in Gary, an important-looking village, and the soldier took her luggage into the office of the District Commander whom she knew. There was a fine porcelain stove in the room, and the table was neatly stacked with folders, papers, and ledgers. The place was empty, but the soldier assured her that the Commander expected her and she would not have long to wait.

She was glad to sit down in a comfortable chair, for her legs ached after the long walk and cramped position on the suitcase. She must have dozed in the comforting warmth, for when she looked at the clock again the hands pointed to two.

She tiptoed to the door, but there was no one in the passage outside; there was no sound of anyone in the adjoining room . . . the silence was oppressive and she felt hungry and hurt at this casual manner of her reception.

Tucked in her rug was a bit of paper containing a slice of bread. She took it out, but it was hard as stone, and would have broken her teeth to eat it. She put it on the stove, hoping to thaw it a little, but even after an hour its saw-like edges were no softer. She could have cried with hunger and fatigue and the complete disregard for the individual which characterized this treatment. Soon it was so dark that she could no longer see the clock. It seemed ages afterwards that the Commander came into the room. He lit a kerosene lamp and seemed confused when he saw her sitting in his chair.

"I was unexpectedly detained," he murmured. "I am sorry you have had to wait for me."

Olga's courage rose with her hunger.

"I have been waiting altogether too long," she complained. "I am tired and cold, and I want some hot food."

He looked surprised at her tone.

"Have you received any money, or the ticket for your journey?" he asked.

"I have received nothing," she burst out passionately. "I have been told nothing—brought here like a parcel —but since the error of my arrest is yours, you will have to furnish me with means to return. It is up to you to take me to my Consulate." She felt that she was at the end of her resources, and knew that in another moment she would be crying like a child.

The District Commander hesitated a few seconds, then looked at her kindly.

"All right," he said, "I'll see about that. Now I'll take you to my wife, and she will give you something to eat."

These were the first words she had ever heard from an official that expressed the least inkling of human feeling, and they almost broke down her self-control.

He took her bags, and walked across the village square, and she followed, the snow creaking and grinding under her feet. He let himself into a one-story house, and took her into a warm room, where a pleasant-looking woman was playing with five or six little children.

"We are having a party," she explained, when her husband introduced Olga. "My little son is five today." She indicated a pretty little boy dressed in a new soldier's uniform, with a tiny sword at his side. Her voice, her manner and the aspect of the room all told Olga that here was another world.

It was little more than a large log cabin, but beautifully kept and full of colour; the floor was stained and polished and there were bright rugs scattered over it.

Though the furniture was simple, and a large bed in one corner suggested that this was the only room in the place, the atmosphere was like that of an artist's studio rather than the bleak horror of the cabin rooms to which Olga had been accustomed.

The woman was settling the children at a long table at one end of the room, and serving them soup and *piroshkis* . . . little hot meat pies. "Let me give you some of these," she said, turning to her newly arrived guest. And for the first time in five months Olga tasted something other than prison fare.

She ate slowly and gratefully, savouring to the utmost the warmth, the delicious food, moved almost to tears by the gracious spirit of the place.

"These are human beings," she thought; "this is how human beings behave . . . in camp we weren't human."

The heat was beginning to make her sleepy . . . in the distance the children were singing songs together . . . about the great Soviet Union and the powerful Red Army (here they all waved their swords) . . . and about the Christmas-tree holiday . . . a long saga of how they went to the forest and cut the tree, and decorated the tree and danced round the tree . . . the wonderful tree which would furnish such good wood . . . for so many useful things. . . . Her head nodded drowsily. And soon the children were going home; then the Commander came back and other guests arrived. Someone turned on a gramophone, and couples danced together. The Commander danced and looked very young and handsome in his fine uniform. His wife sat by Olga's side, asking her about her life in Poland,

and her "adventures," taking a kindly interest in her forthcoming trip. She and her husband came from Leningrad, she said; and from the tone of her conversation, Olga felt perfectly sure that their transfer to this obscure post at Gary meant that they were expiating some deviation from the Party "line."

The hostess and another woman set the table for supper; and then everyone sat down to a large dish of lamb stew. Olga had never tasted such succulent meat: it seemed unbelievable that she should be eating again, and sitting so comfortably with knives and forks and pretty crockery before her. On the table were dishes of pickled herring and cheese: the guests chatted and helped themselves; there was hot tea and vodka to drink, and afterwards the Commander's wife opened a big box of candy. Olga had forgotten there could be such plenty; she felt she had come to an unreal world.

When supper was cleared away the Commander took a violin case out of a bureau drawer.

"Are you really a musician?" he asked. "Was it true when you told me you could play the violin?"

He handed her the instrument as though putting her to a test; but as she took it in her hand she had to shut her eyes to fight down the smothering rush of emotions that threatened to choke her. She swayed dizzily in silence as everyone waited for her to begin. Then she lifted it to her chin. Her fingertips were cracked and maimed; her hands swollen with broken chilblains, the delicate muscles stiff and ruined; her right arm still painful and almost useless from the recent fall. But she drew the bow across the strings with a mastery that electrified her hearers as she played a song of Sarasate.

The Commander did not say one word as she handed the violin back to him. From the way he handled it and the manner in which his fingers lingered on the shining surface she knew he loved it, however, and her heart softened a little towards him.

"Do you play?" she asked, briefly.

"A little," he admitted.

He played a simple air. His tone was clean enough but his technique so poor, so clumsy, she knew he had never studied with a good teacher. An immense bitterness overcame her. "They set me to haul wood," she thought. "They destroyed my hands with useless manual labour, and I could have brought music to their villages and taught those who care for lovely things. The waste . . . the waste!" She choked back a sob.

Everyone begged her to play again, but she was too tired, too resentful, to make the effort.

She leaned back exhausted in her chair, while the others sat around the stove, talking, smoking, and laughing in low tones. Most of the men were in uniform; the women, in sweaters and skirts, were shabby, though not ill-favoured. On the bed sat the little boy. He had pulled Olga's umbrella from the roll of rugs and was playing with it, opening and shutting it, completely fascinated with this absorbing toy. "I have never seen such a funny thing," he said, wonder in his eyes.

The guests left about half past eleven and the Commander's wife put the little boy to sleep in the big bed. She arranged his cot with blankets for Olga and the Commander suggested that she lie down for an hour before continuing her journey.

"I am driving you to Sosva, where we shall get the train for Siroff," he explained.

The names meant nothing to her, though she wondered wearily if Russians ever made a journey that did not necessitate setting out in the middle of the night!

At twelve-thirty he roused her, helped her into her coat, and tip-toed out of the room, putting her bags into a heavy open truck.

She stood in this, clutching the sides as they lurched through the sleeping village and out into the frozen path that cut a white streak through the forest. Once the Commander put his arm on hers, pointing at two eyes that glittered up at them from among the trees. Then he turned the head-lights full on the animal and it slunk back into the darkness.

"We get a lot of wolves in winter," he whispered.

She was too tired to be frightened, too tired to notice which way they were going. It seemed hours before they stopped, and she found herself following the Commander along a snowy path in the direction of a dark gloomy building. Three steps covered with thick ice led to the front door; she stumbled up and would have fallen if he had not caught her.

"Whatever is this place?" she thought wildly, as they entered a large room lit by a guttering kerosene lamp, and saw on the ground scores of people, men, women, and children sprawling in attitudes of uneasy sleep. Everything was still and ghostlike, except for grunts and groans of the sleepers wrapped in their sheepskins and surrounded by litter. There was a fetid stench of food remains, urine, old newspapers and unwashed feet.

"We have to stay here for a bit," said the Commander, rather apologetically, as he found an empty corner for her suitcase, and settled her as comfortably as he could.

Afterwards she thought it must have been some kind of waiting-room behind the station, for when they left on the train some hours later it seemed to her that they did not go far before they clambered into a third-class compartment.

Trains never ran on schedule, she remembered; they were due when they arrived. People always camped on the platform until something with a few empty cars came along in the direction they wanted to go. New Soviet regulations had tried to clear this unsightly crowd out of view, but it was still there in the background, eating and sleeping amid its myriad packages, waiting patiently till the conductor, at some preceding station, telegraphed ahead to say how many more passengers he could squeeze into the crowded cars.

She drowsed on the hard, wooden seat as the train bounced tinnily along; and next day, for breakfast, a young man shared some black bread with her. She waited an hour and a half at Siroff while the District Commander did a great deal of telephoning and spoke with the railway officials, making arrangements for the rest of the trip.

Olga looked about her with interest. Siroff was a fairly large station, a two-storied construction of heavy, squared logs, with a waiting room and restaurant, and an outside counter where a girl sold soft drinks of cranberry juice and water. The platform, enclosed by a high picket fence, was deep in snow, with a fir tree or two growing at each end, and completely deserted, though the sun was shining as brilliantly as in a mountain resort. Inside the waiting room a couple of Secret Police officers watched Olga closely; they walked all round her, noting her coat and shoes, taking stock of every detail of her attire. She was amused at first by their attentions, their so obvious suspicions.

"Take a good look at me," she thought. "Maybe I'm an escaping prisoner . . . keep your eyes on me. . . ." Impressed by her cool unconcern, one of them wandered away, but the other continued his solitary watch, never ceasing to stare at her and occasionally walking round and round her.

"I've just as much right to be here as you!" she felt like saying to him, annoyed at last by his impertinence.

She glanced at the portraits of Stalin which decorated the walls, and the faded photographs of Red Army manœuvres tacked up everywhere. A few passengers were eating in the restaurant: in their old-fashioned clothes, amid that primitive setting, the scene reminded her of an American country railway station in the early 'nineties.

The District Commander came back at last, handing her a ticket.

"You get the train to Sverdlovsk here," he said, picking up her baggage and carrying it onto the platform. "At Sverdlovsk you will be met by two N.K.W.D. officers, who will put you on the Trans-Siberian Express for Moscow."

"But how will they recognize me?" queried Olga, fearful of missing the connection at this big Siberian junction.

"They'll know you," answered the Commander, and

his tones were so quietly ominous that Olga had the impression that no stranger ever went unwatched in Russia.

"From now on you will be either in a train or a covered station, so I will take the fur coat back to Steputin," he added. She hated to give it up: even over her own wool coat, it had not been a bit too warm. But she realized it would have been impossible to have returned it to its owner from any other place, so she gave it to the Commander together with the *czunias* and a note for Mrs. Altberg.

"I want to thank you for all your kindness," she began. The District Commander shook her warmly by the hand. For the first time she felt that here was someone who was genuinely sorry for all her experiences.

"Good-bye, good luck!" he said, putting her on the train, and smiling very kindly at her.

"Good-bye . . . and specially good luck to you!" she called, as it moved out of the station.

It was not very comfortable, that trip to Sverdlovsk. The train was unheated, and the big, draughty section with its hard, wooden seats grew terribly cold as the hours went by. But a long-haired peasant in a sheepskin coat and high boots, looking exactly like something out of a White Russian cabaret, drew sweet music from an accordion and all the other passengers begged to be allowed to play, so there was music and singing the whole time.

And true enough, at Sverdlovsk Olga had hardly descended from the train when two officers from the Secret Police were standing beside her.

"Are you Kochanska?" they asked immediately.

They took her into the waiting room and examined her ticket, which they forthwith pronounced as being "not in order."

"You will have to buy another," they commanded.

"But I have no money," she objected.

There was more elaborate telephoning to some mysterious source of authority. But Olga refused to accept any responsibility for her expenses.

"You brought me here, you must get me out of here!" she kept repeating sweetly.

Finally they bought her a third-class ticket to Moscow, and gave her sixty-five roubles for pocket money for the trip. She immediately went into the restaurant and bought a cup of coffee. She was beginning to enjoy her travels. She sat at a table, slowly sipping the delicious brew, taking in the crowded scene with great relish. The station restaurant was full; passengers kept coming and going through the big swing doors from the platforms, eating at the counters heavily laden with dishes of pickled fish, chopped meats, beet salads, cheese, different kinds of bread.

Everyone was extremely solemn. Though the crowd did not lack movement and variety, there was no talking or animation; it was uniformly dingy and ill-clad, and she could not remember having seen such a glum-looking set of tourists anywhere before. "At least not outside a prison convoy," she added, thinking of her own ghastly trip.

With plenty of time to spare, and money in her pocket, she treated herself to a second cup of coffee. It cost a rouble a cup: an untold extravagance, but it was such a sweet luxury, one of the things she had missed most in camp. She had often dreamed of the moment when she would taste her first cup of coffee; it had become an obsession with her, second only to her longing for candy, and far outstripping any desire for food. She drained the last drop, only wishing that by some magic she could send a lot of it to camp. (Shall I ever really enjoy anything while they are still there? she wondered.) Then she went onto the platform to wait for the Moscow train.

Two days and nights she rode "hard," with a wooden bunk to sleep on and no covers, for third-class passengers are supposed to bring their own bedding. An elderly officer, a major in the Red Army, snored on the opposite berth, for a Russian sleeping-car is no respecter of sexes. From time to time during the long trip they exchanged desultory remarks, though after her experiences of Soviet rule, Olga found his complacency regarding its perfection and the rotten condition of all other countries (he had never been outside Russia) hard to stomach. Once or twice a day the *provodnik*, or official in charge of the coach, brought hot water for all those who carried teakettles; and when the refuse on the floor—the cheese rinds, eggshells and greasy paper—grew too thick, he made perfunctory movements with a broom, sweeping most of the litter into the four corners of the compartment.

There had been no bookstand or newspaper kiosk at Sverdlovsk, so Olga had nothing with her to read. The windows were coated with ice. Idly she turned out her handbag, arranging its contents. She came across a letter she had forgotten, sent to her in camp from a friend in the Russian-held land which had once been Poland. The envelope bore a Jubilee stamp, a fine design of a Bolshevik tank and an armed Red soldier, with two peasants' heads in the foreground. A flamboyant inscription bordered it: "Liberation of the brother nations, Ukraine and Ruthenia, 17/9/'39."

Staring from the sluttish coupé to the tiny picture, her thoughts grew bitter as the Soviet symbols burned themselves in her mind.

"What does Russian 'liberation' mean to the peoples who get it?" she pondered. "If only those who clamour for Communism could come and see it in action . . . on the spot, the grinding daily tyranny . . . the incompetence and inefficiency . . . the whole flimsy structure of planned economy applied to verminous, illiterate poverty. And it was through fear of this . . . this slum clearance," she concluded, with cold, growing anger, "that the world allowed Hitler to grow great!"

To the Russian officer she related some of her camp experiences and asked him why the Soviet régime was deporting so many Poles to Siberia.

"Well . . . if they are innocent people they'll get out," he stated categorically. "The innocent will go free."

"But think of the awful conditions," objected Olga. "They might die."

The man fixed her with a cold stare that reminded her of Steputin. "That's what they're there for," he remarked bluntly.

She got up and left the compartment; she could no longer tolerate the company of such a man. She told the *provodnik* to move her suitcase into another section, which she shared with a young nurse who was taking a patient to Moscow for treatment. The girl was kindly, competent, big-eyed. "You should stay on in Moscow," she urged, when she learned something of Olga's story; "you could earn a lot of money teaching English and violin there . . . you don't know how much we need those things. . . ."

But Olga stayed in Moscow only long enough to see her Consul, and get an exit visa. She had no desire to linger and heaved a sigh of relief when she found herself once more on the Trans-Siberian, bound this time for the Pacific.

From the frozen double windows she could see little of the monotonous landscape, nor did she wish to look. It recalled too vividly her other long journey and the martyrdom of her exodus from Poland. When glimpses of snow-clad forest flashed by, her heart sank as she remembered her comrades still imprisoned in their lonely cabins; when she got out at the stations to walk and buy food, their starving faces haunted her.

Her fellow-travellers, a doctor from Budapest, a Bulgarian, a Swedish lady, were congenial companions; the days passed quickly as they read and talked together in English . . . but she could not banish the burden of her memories. Would she ever enjoy real freedom after all that she had gone through, after all that she knew?

At Omsk, where they paced the platform one early morning, the temperature was fifty-five below zero; yet as they moved out of the station they saw cattle trucks in which Russian workmen and workgirls stood packed in serried ranks, waiting to be taken to their job down the line. They were not prisoners, but well-paid factory operatives. "Let's hope they are not going far." Olga shuddered, remembering her own trip in a cattle truck . . . though she realized now that this was "fourth-class" travel, and not considered an infamy.

The Trans-Siberian cut a thin line across the world's storehouse of timber on either side of the tracks. As far as Olga could see, the land seemed hardly scratched. Cities were hundreds of miles apart and only at river junctions; here and there a road meandered a few miles, then vanished in the immense distances; little townships of huddled log buildings sprang to sight, too small to be marked on any map, their grey-painted window-frames whittled and fretted in intricate designs, the work of interminable winters, each village fenced with high timber and huge, padlocked gates, a veritable fortress against wolves.

After the train left Omsk it plunged into the Taiga —that vast tract of primeval forest, a boundary line between two worlds—where titan trunks jostled each other and struggled to emerge from the solid vegetation; that irresistible monster growth which has consumed all its rivals, has swallowed whole herds of mammoth, fought the glaciers and overcome them, and successfully defeated man's feeble attempt to tame it.

Olga turned from her peephole in the frozen window-panes with a shiver; the sight was too desolate, too gloomly reminiscent of the one from which she had but recently escaped.

Two Russian officers wearing the highest military orders on their dark blue uniforms had entered the train and were ordering champagne in the dining car.

Each day of the trip they celebrated their return from Finland, and pressed champagne upon Olga and her companions. They drank and talked incessantly; they were, they admitted, *nalemonetzia,* or "full of little lemons," which Olga translated to the Hungarian as "pie-eyed." One of them had brought back from Finland a pair of maral horns, a priceless trophy, for they were "in velvet" and consequently possessed the magic quality of making old men young.

"You grind them to powder and boil them in salt," explained the officer. "Then there is a secret process, but the effects can be guaranteed. Russia did a big business in maral horns at one time," continued the lucky owner. "Ruined now, of course," he sighed. "We used to get any price we asked for them—it was mostly with China . . . those marvellous old mandarins with all their concubines . . . !"

The officer who spoke was a Siberian, from Tobolsk; his people had once been peasant millionaires there, fisherfolk who worked at their trade side by side with their own workmen, and who, when the salmon came up the river, could hardly cope with the glut of the stupendous catches. They were a lusty, simple lot, all members of the family, sometimes three and four generations, sleeping together in one great room—for separate bedrooms were an unknown luxury. And in poor families, animals shared the house as well, and in winter many a hencoop served as a table in the large kitchen-parlor.

Olga listened to their tales in silence. For her, the enforced co-habitation had been the most humiliating

part of her long imprisonment, but the Siberians found
it perfectly natural.

At Irkutsk tall buildings of brick and concrete rose in
sight, the Governor's palace, the dome of a church,
grim satanic factories. This was the town of hard-riding,
hard-swearing Cossacks, said the officers: a city with
reckless blood in its veins, which had grown to wealth
by looting geographical secrets from nature, and piled
up fortunes from the gold strikes and tea cavarans of
China. From hectic buying and selling of millions in
crude, log-walled cabins, its citizens had built the railway line that linked the Baltic with the Pacific, had become the great industrialists of the Soviet Union. . . .

"To the glory of Irkutsk!" shouted the officers, lifting their champagne glasses in a toast.

"And mind you watch out for Baikal," they boasted,
"the deepest lake in the world . . . with strange precious stones on its shores, and strange creatures in and
under its surface, and stranger people roaming its
forests. . . ."

Late into the night Olga waited, straining for sight
of the great frozen waterway. The train threaded in-
numerable tunnels, where giant icicles hung like mighty
stalactites; but it was noon next day before she caught
her first glimpse of its scimitar-shaped shores. Precipitous cliffs rose darkly about its queer outline, this lake
which is as long as England and formed volcanically
by a cataclysmic explosion which ripped open the
earth's crust along the Angara River.

"There is no other land like this in all the world,"
dilated the enthusiastic officer. "It has never at any

time of its existence been covered by the ocean; it's probably the most ancient region known to man!"

He took personal satisfaction in the antiquity of the soil, and counted like a child the eighty-one tunnels skirting the lakeside. Nor did his native pride seem the least bit dashed by the gradual lack of amenities the country revealed on its steady passage eastwards. It did not embarrass him that, after Sverdlovsk, station restaurants offered no other food but bread for sale to travellers; or that at some stations peasant women and children came to the train and begged for something to eat.

It was the picture of these hungry, shawl-huddled figures that lingered longest in Olga's memory of all the six-thousand miles of Soviet territory . . . that, and the phlegmatic pack-camels waiting in the snow outside Petrovsk, last reminder of Asia's ancient grip on Russia.

The grinding crash of waves on the arid rocks of the Pacific announced the end of the railway journey, but there were still thousands of foreign miles between her and the freedom she longed for.

Japan seemed hardly real to her—an exquisite etching in green and sepia. The elegant compactness of native life entranced her; yet the unspontaneous politeness and suggestion of censored behaviour marred casual contacts, making them utterly alien.

Not till she descended at Honolulu did the scene feel familiar and she knew she was on the home-stretch. These people were free; the fact was gloriously self-evident the moment she stepped off the ship. She wandered through busy thoroughfares, lost in admiration of the happy, beautifully dressed crowds, watched the careless spending in opulent shops, stood spell-bound before the forgotten magnificence of a five-and-ten-cent store! Such a wealth of purchasable commodities, after the barren products of Russia's Five Years' Plan, appeared little short of miraculous . . . everything was so well-made, so ingenious, so incredibly cheap. Visions of her barter with Siberian peasants rose before her, and of the clumsy pocket-knife in a Moscow store priced sixty-five roubles . . . almost half a man's monthly wages.

"With the contents of Honolulu," she felt like concluding, "you could buy all Russia!"

But at home in Chicago even such calculations faded and she forgot to make comparisons.

Here, for the first time since her release, she was able to slip the yoke of her memories, for here, as she had often dreamed it, hardly daring to believe it would ever happen, yet never ceasing to pray for its coming, here was a letter from England, a letter from her own boy Jan.

She forgot her own fate and the record of her sufferings as she read the incredible story her son had to tell.

Sole survivor of a cavalry regiment that charged a German tank corps, twice taken prisoner and twice evading his captors, fighting as long as a Poland existed to fight in, threatened with death, hunted, but returning to Warsaw in spite of the German occupation, hidden by friends, he managed to save and secrete treasures dear to them both in their home there. He witnessed the awful plight and material losses of his country, heard of death and execution of friends and best-loved comrades; then away, with only his strength and courage to help him, through neighbouring countries with hairbreadth adventures, resisting in France till the end came, and on with the British to fight the war to a finish, to wait for a day of reckoning. . . .

"I will avenge; I will avenge my country's sufferings," he wrote. "I will avenge Hitler's blasphemous savagery, his brutish aggression and merciless treatment of our people. I will avenge." It was the cry from the hearts of thousands of young Poles who had witnessed the violation of their land by Germany's perfectly functioning military machine.

In this new, stern figure, this politically aroused captain of cavalry, Olga hardly recognized the sensitive, beauty-loving youth she had known. Only the simplicity and warmth of his words to her meant that in his personal relations her Johnny had not changed.

Her own sufferings and the conclusions she had drawn paled before the burning indignation of his wider experiences. It was but natural that her resentment should have been focussed in a different direction, yet even Olga had never regarded Russians and Germans in the same light. Jan's letter re-established her perspective—one which history endorsed as well. She knew that for centuries Poles and Russians had fought each other without ever destroying their recognition of a bond of kinship. More than a hundred years before, Pushkin had addressed one of his most beautiful poems to those who raged at Russians for persecuting Poles, much as they have done today:

Back safely in her native land, where national loyalties are not challenged by century-old disputes, Olga found that time was healing her resentment. And when German fury turned at last on Russia, the matter was clinched for her: indignation at her personal tribulations dwindled before the realization of what grim fate her adopted country faced were Germany to remain the victor.

Then, too, she was no longer tormented by thoughts of her warm-hearted friends in prison. They would be given their freedom now. The settlement between Poland and Russia, resulting from this last aggression, meant that the exiles from Lemberg would be released from that dreary concentration camp—genial Josef

* *To the Slanderers of Russia.* Translation by Eugene de Savitsch, M.D.

Fischer, who hid his fears for his wife's sake; querulous kindly Dr. Altberg; the plucky women who would not give in; the old folk, their eyes full of wistful longing; the defiant indomitable children—their misery was ended. The Soviet-Polish Agreement set them free!

How would they take the news of their deliverance? Could they forget old rancours, decide to start life anew? Would it be possible?

Olga knew little enough of psychology and nothing of politics or the economic aspects of the case. But she possessed wisdom born of faith in imperishable things, nature, beauty—the wisdom of artists and poets.

Looking back at the gallant souls of Zimny Gorodok, she knew what Pushkin meant. Courage like theirs is never useless; and where it exists a nation cannot die.

Bear Trap Farm
Mount Solon, Virginia
August, 1941.

www.ingramcontent.com/pod-product-compliance
Lightning Source LLC
Chambersburg PA
CBHW071400150726
48000CB00001B/110